PRAISE FOR

IF ENGAGEMENT IS
THE WHAT, THEN RESPECT
IS THE HOW

This book should be required reading for anyone in a leadership position in any type of organization. You'll come away understanding how critically important Employee Engagement is to the achievement of personal and business objectives. And John Guaspari's writing style and wit make it an easy and enjoyable read.

WALTER I. FLAHERTY, COO AND CFO, NEW
ENGLAND AQUARIUM (RET.)

Once again, John Guaspari has chosen a weighty and yet soft subject that all companies must try to wrap their arms around in their search for success. He combines research and wit to engage his readers and help them learn how to use the "soft" intangibles that lead to the "hard" numbers all leaders seek at the end of each quarter.

This book should be used as a handbook for onboarding sessions to give new employees an understanding of what a company values and how it could help them achieve their personal and company goals.

My only wish is that Guaspari had pointed us to the Mirror Company that could be the supplier of the key tool he recommends along the path to higher levels of Employee Engagement and the dramatically improved business results they can provide.

PAM MADDALENA, SENIOR VICE PRESIDENT
HUMAN RELATIONS, PORTER NOVELLI (RET.)

John Guaspari's latest book—*If Engagement is the What, Then Respect is the How*—combines his trademark wit with the kind of deft reasoning that strips away your defenses. He's like a master logician that you'd want on your debate team for both the win and the laughs. He has peeled back today's buzzwords down to their essence: Empowerment is about safety, Trust is earned. And he uses candid examples to guide his readers to the unavoidable conclusion that Respect is the fuel that drives every good organization. A powerfully true take on how to grasp the intangibles of success.

ELISABETH SWAN, AUTHOR OF *PICTURE YOURSELF A LEADER*

A great read, well-structured with a logic I found compelling. And the writing is superb. Sage advice that will deliver tangible results.

GERALD DUNDON, VP GLOBAL LOGISTICS AND PLANNING, ANALOG DEVICES INC. (RET.)

IF ENGAGEMENT IS THE WHAT, THEN RESPECT IS THE HOW

HARD-LEARNED LESSONS FROM DEALING WITH THOSE PESKY INTANGIBLES, A.K.A., "THE SOFT STUFF"

IF ENGAGEMENT IS THE WHAT, THEN RESPECT IS THE HOW

HARD-LEARNED LESSONS FROM DEALING WITH THOSE PESKY INTANGIBLES, A.K.A., "THE SOFT STUFF"

JOHN GUASPARI

FAIRWAYS PUBLICATIONS

OTHER BOOKS BY JOHN GUASPARI

I Know It When I See It:
A Modern Fable About Quality

Theory Why:
In Which the Boss Solves the Riddle of Quality

The Customer Connection:
Quality For the Rest of Us

It's About Time:
A Fable About the Next Dimension of Quality

Switched-On Quality:
How to Tap Into the Energy Needed
for Fuller and Deeper Buy-In

The Value Effect:
A Murder Mystery About the Compulsive
Pursuit of "The Next Big Thing"

Otherwise Engaged:
How Leaders Can Get a Firmer Grip on
Employee Engagement and Other Key Intangibles

DEDICATION

My first book was published in 1985. I was surprised that I wrote it, amazed that I found a publisher for it, and stunned that it sold well. Well enough, in fact, to precipitate my entry into the world of management consulting.

Six more books, seven training videos, hundreds of articles and columns and speeches and seminars, and work with scores of clients later, and I could look back on a pretty successful career before retiring from full-time consulting work in 2013, the last ten years of which was as an internal consultant for a Fortune 200 company.

Back to that first book. Its dedication read, simply, **For Gail.**

Gail was my wife. The past tense in that last sentence indicates, sadly, that she died in 2020, shortly after our fortieth wedding anniversary. I didn't realize how prescient that two-word dedication would be, since that "pretty successful career" meant a lot of time on the road, which is to say, a lot of time away from Gail and our two kids.

Gail was a stay-at-home mom, and she was also wonderful at it, as is borne out by our two now-very-much-adult children.

None of this—my pretty successful career, our very-much-adult children, my memories of forty blessed years of marriage—could have happened without Gail's warmth and passion and love and humor and devotion to all of us.

So, the dedication for this book can only be one thing, which is, once again...**For Gail.**

CONTENTS

PREFACE

WHAT YOU'LL BE READING ABOUT IN THESE PAGES

There's no question about it. If all that was involved was keeping projects on time and on budget and everything was reduceable to neat rows and columns on a spreadsheet and snazzy PowerPoint presentations that flowed seamlessly into your KPIs, then leadership would be a lot simpler.

WHAT COMPLICATES MATTERS IS THAT YOU HAVE TO DO ALL THIS STUFF THROUGH THOSE HIGHLY VARIABLE THINGS CALLED…PEOPLE.

People who come from different backgrounds. People who have different outlooks on things. People with different skill sets—and different degrees of competence within those skill sets. People who are motivated by different incentive structures. And maybe even some people who aren't so sure they want to be there at all.

That makes things kind of tricky. But you still have to deal with it if you're going to be a successful leader. Yet as we all know, it's all those Intangibles—a.k.a., the Soft Stuff—that's the hard part. In this very short book, I will attempt to demystify some of those Intangibles by writing about them in simple, straightforward language.

The focal point will be on employee Engagement, since one of the most important things you can do to ensure the success of your company (or your division (or your team)) is to ensure that people are as fully engaged in the tasks at hand as possible.

Engagement ought to be *the* critical focus of your people-efforts as a leader: the *What* of the challenge, if you will.

The problem is that the way many organizations (and divisions (and teams)) try to achieve high levels of Engagement is—not to put too fine a point on things—wrong. I'll write about that, too, and how to avoid this pitfall.

One of the waystations toward Engagement is Empowerment. It, too, is important, but the way it's gone about is also too often—yup—wrong. I'll cover that as well.

Another waystation is Trust. This one is a little different, because unlike Engagement and Empowerment, which sound like they were coined in a corporate laboratory, Trust is something we've heard about all our lives. I'm going to write about Trust and offer some thoughts about how it ought to be handled—which is really just a gentler way of saying that *it's* often handled in the wrong way too.

That brings us to Respect. It, too, is something we've heard about all our lives. All of us know what it feels like to be respected or disrespected. All of us may or may not treat other people with respect at times. We often bollox this one up as well, and I'll offer some thoughts to explain how and why that happens.

The point I want to emphasize here, though, is the special role that Respect has in this context, since it is the one Intangible over which we have control...that focusing on infusing Respect—each of us, all day, every day, in our dealings with other people—is the *How* when it comes to maximizing Engagement levels.

The argument I'm going to make in this book, therefore, is this:

Higher levels of Engagement is
***What* you should be striving to achieve.**

**Infusing higher levels of Respect throughout
your organization is *How* to achieve it.**

As I said, it's a short book. Partly that's because I know people are busy and don't have a lot of time to read. Mostly, though, it's because these concepts, properly understood, ought to be elucidated in quick, straightforward language. There's no need to lard it up with a lot of woo-woo theory.

But—full disclosure—I also have an insidious motive. My goal is to make things so clear and irrefutable that it strips away your defenses so that you're left with no choice but to come to grips with those heretofore inscrutable Intangibles.

If, that is, it were possible to grip an intangible.

———

A bit more about what's contained in these pages. My last book was published in 2015 and was titled *Otherwise Engaged: How Leaders Can Get a Firmer Grip on Employee Engagement and Other Key Intangibles (If, That Is, It Were Possible to Grip Something That's Intangible)*.

You'll notice that the language in that subtitle sounds a lot like some of the language I just used above. That's hardly an accident. You see, in my last book, I tried to get too cute. Instead of just laying out the case I had to make about Engagement and Respect and the other Intangibles, I thought it would be more effective if I illustrated those points by interweaving the more didactic chapters with chapters telling the story of how a well-meaning but ill-advised management consultant tried to apply his consulting techniques to achieve higher levels of Engagement, Respect, and so on, in his family. I thought it would be a fun and funny way to break up the serious bits.

Instead, though, the family's story turned out to be a distraction. Readers wanted to get on to the serious bits and found themselves annoyed at having to read about the family's travails.[1]

So what I've done in this book, essentially, was to strip out the family story from *Otherwise Engaged* and preserve the so-called serious bits, with some trimming and adding along the way. My hope is that this more straight-line approach to making the case for Engagement, Respect, et. al., will prove to be more effective and, therefore, more valuable to you, the reader.

---

1. Some of which were, dammit, fun and funny.

INTRODUCTION

"Leadership is the art of getting someone else to do what
you want done because he wants to do it."

GENERAL DWIGHT D. EISENHOWER

This book is about leadership, the defining characteristic of which is
the existence of followers. For our purposes, "leader" can mean C-level
executives, or it can mean frontline supervisors. It can mean a person
with explicit positional authority over a business unit of a Fortune 100
company as well as someone called on to head up an eight-person, ad
hoc project team who must lead through influence alone.

It's also about "Engagement," a concept that is front-and-center on
more and more leaders' screens these days. And that's for very good
reasons. Compelling research done by multiple reputable sources
demonstrates the indisputable correlation between high levels of
Employee Engagement and substantially improved business results as
measured along such critical dimensions as profitability, productivity,
and employee retention rates.

Engagement doesn't happen in a vacuum, though. Focusing on it inevitably means coming face-to-face with such related matters as Empowerment, Trust, and Respect, a.k.a., "The Soft Stuff." The people stuff.

Attending to all of this effectively is a nontrivial challenge. But leaders don't become leaders by backing down when faced with such challenges. They take action—the *summum bonum* of complex organizational life—by launching serious-minded, well-funded initiatives to drive up Engagement levels, appropriately genuflecting along the way to Engagement's first cousins, the other Intangibles. Leaders do their homework, researching the currently accepted tools and techniques, settling not just for any practices, but only for *best* practices.

It's all very sensible, logical, and rational…and often as not, the results come up short of expectations. So the question becomes: Why?

It's a question I tried to help leaders in hundreds of organizations representing scores of industries answer during my years as a consultant. During that career, there were two incidents that brightly illuminated just what the answer might be.

HERE'S ONE OF THEM.

I was standing on the stage of a corporate auditorium. The title of the presentation I was about to make was the standard one I used in such instances: "Making the Business Case for 'The Intangibles.'" If you were to try to imagine a group of people more predisposed to be skeptical about this sort of subject matter, you'd be hard pressed to come up with a better one than the hundred or so people I was facing at that moment: the security team of a business unit of a major technology company. Suffice it to say, these were not people whose schedules tended to be overfilled with matters pertaining to soft stuff.

A few days earlier, I had told a colleague that this assignment would be a piece of cake: "All I have to do is make a logical, left-brained argument to an overwhelmingly logical, left-brained audience that logical, left-brained arguments aren't enough." I was joking, but I also knew that this pretty well captured the essence of the challenge before me.

I believed that what I had to say had the potential to be of considerable value, even to such logical, left-brained folks. That wouldn't be the case, though, unless I could find a way to get past the Starship Enterprise-grade deflector shields that such audiences reflexively deploy—set to eleven—when under threat of bombardment by what they perceived to be such Kumbaya-ish subject matter.

So I took a risk. Instead of beginning my presentation by talking *about* the Intangibles, I decided to try to get them to vicariously *feel* one.

I began by telling them the story of what happened on the evening our son Mike was born, some thirty years earlier. I described my wife Gail announcing that the big moment had arrived…the phone calls to the hospital and obstetrician… the gathering up of the go-bags… the short/long four-mile drive to the hospital. I told them of how the song that happened to be playing on the car radio when I turned the ignition key was Billy Joel's "Piano Man"… that by the end of the song, we had arrived at the hospital…that by the end of the night mother and baby were doing great.

Here's how I concluded the story: "To this day, whenever I hear 'Piano Man,' I get a powerful emotional jolt. I cannot prove it to you. I cannot show it to you. I cannot put it in front of you so that you can touch it or taste it or smell it. But don't you *dare* try to tell me that this feeling is not real. What's more, everyone in this room has an equivalent story to tell…about something that will trigger a deeply rooted bit of sense memory and give you that same kind of emotional jolt. That's what I mean by the 'Intangibles.' That's what we're going to be talking about for the next hour or so."

I could tell by the body language in the room that it had worked, that their deflector shields had come down. Most of all, I could tell when, at the end of the hour, I thanked them for their time and attention and exited stage left, at which point one of those oh-so-logical/rational security professionals held up his iPhone—volume cranked up to eleven—and serenaded us all with Billy Joel's "Piano Man." That was one of the most gratifying moments of my professional career.

What happened next, however, was not.

A fifteen-minute break was called, and a human resources director for the business unit approached me.

"May I offer you some constructive feedback?" she asked.

"Of course," I replied.

"This is a pretty diverse group," she said. "Not all of them are baby boomers like you and I are. So their tastes in music are likely to be different from ours. I think your story would have been more effective if instead of using a song by Billy Joel you had used one by someone like, say, Katy Perry."

What I said in reply was this: "Hmm. Interesting point. I'll be sure to give it some thought."

What I had wanted to say was this: "But what I said was, like, what actually happened. 'Piano Man' is the song that was *on the radio!* An hour ago, I stood up in front of these people and opened a vein and shared a *deeply personal, deeply emotional story.* One that I had never shared in public before. I understand that this is a diverse team and that, Lord knows, they're all the stronger as a result. *But 'Piano Man' is what was on the radio that night! And besides which, KATY PERRY IS YOUNGER THAN MIKE!"*

All of which goes to prove yet again that attempting to deal with the Intangibles is like trying to lasso a cloud. Don't get me wrong. I am more than prepared to concede that she may have missed the point of the "Piano Man" story because of my shortcomings as a presenter. But the guy who held up the iPhone seemed to get it. So, too, did all of the people who sang along to "Piano Man" when he did. So how was it that a human resources director—*a human resources director*—didn't?

I think it has to do with the fact that leaders have a strong bias toward logical, rational, data-driven solutions to problems. It's a bias that is reinforced by the dynamic push and pull of organizational life. You don't become a leader—or at least you won't be a leader for long—by relying on gut feel and emotion alone.

For the record, I am not immune to the appeal of such a worldview. Both my undergraduate and graduate degrees are in aerospace engineering, and I spent the first few years of my career in that profession. I, too, like to be data-driven.

But doesn't the fact that so many well-intentioned initiatives fall short of expectations represent important data? In what sense are you being data-driven when you come up short and think, "We did our best. But, you know, it's the soft stuff that's the hard part, so..." thereby shrugging away the possibility that maybe the approach that was taken wasn't so sensible and rational after all?

Which brings us to the root of the problem, and I think it has to do with the fact that security professionals are not the only ones with hair-triggers on their deflector shields. Sad to say, pretty much everybody has them. It's just human nature.

Well-intentioned and sensible though they may be, those rational, well-resourced, best-practice-driven initiatives amount to the application of mechanical, utilitarian prescriptions to what is essentially a problem of the spirit and soul.

It's not that such approaches *don't* work. It's that they _can't_ work, any more than even the most powerful antibiotic will cure a viral infection.

That's a costly problem for businesses, since they invest a lot in what has come to be called their human capital, and there are enormous benefits to be realized by leaders who are able to get a firmer grip on Engagement and the related intangibles... if, that is, it were possible to get a handle on those Intangibles, something that, by definition, can't be touched.

Yep, that's a paradox, and it's what we'll be covering in these pages. Such is the ambiguity of the leader's challenge. Embrace it. You might just as well, since you can't embrace the Intangibles themselves.

1 ULTIMATELY, IT HAS TO DO WITH "BUTTERFLY-NESS"

T he first step in gaining a better "grip"[1] on the Intangibles is to recognize—and even embrace—the fact that the Intangibles are…intangible.

As an intellectual proposition, this is easy enough to accept. It's also easy to accept that the Intangibles are important and that our ability to attend to them effectively affects business results.

As a visceral proposition, though, many (most?) of us have an innate discomfort in dealing with such matters. But we know that we have to "*Do* something!" vis-à-vis the Intangibles, and our strong bias is toward doing the sorts of things that have worked for us in the past.

In the great majority of cases, this is a perfectly rational approach. Unfortunately, though, the Intangibles exist on another plane, one that is not *ir*-rational but that is *extra*-rational, i.e., *other than* rational. And that extra-rational plane is different—profoundly different—from the rational plane. As a matter of fact, it's orthogonal to it, which means

---

1. The quotation marks around "grip" absolve me from the need to add "if it were possible to get a grip on something that's intangible."

that if you're operating on the rational plane, those Intangibles won't be visible to you. They won't even cast a shadow.

TO GET THIS DISCUSSION DOWN OUT OF THE CLOUDS, LET ME POSE A QUESTION.

What is in this picture? (Hint: It's not a trick question.)

Answer: A butterfly.

Another question: **What is in *this* picture?**

Answer: A butterfly.

But while "butterfly" is correct in both cases, the two pictures represent dramatically different things.

The first one shows a butterfly that has been netted, euthanized,[2] pressed, pinned, matted, and framed. It provides very useful informa-

---

2. Picture a bottle of chloroform and a *very* small handkerchief.

tion about the butterfly: its length, width, weight, color, signature wing patterns, and so on—its tangible aspects. So, is it a fair representation of a butterfly? Yes.

But while the second picture isn't as clear about length/width-type attributes, it does a much better job of capturing what, for lack of a better term, might be called the creature's "butterfly-ness." Its "gossamer essence," if you will—an Intangible.

Another question: **Which of the two representations of a butterfly is more useful in practice?**

The answer? It depends.

If you're a lepidopterist doing research, you'd probably get more useful information from the netted/euthanized/pinned/matted/framed picture. If you're a poet, the butterfly alighted on a flower in a meadow would likely provide more inspiration as you plied your trade.

Yet another question: **As a businessperson, which sorts of things are you more comfortable dealing with?**

a. Things like length, width, weight, color, signature wing patterns?
b. Or things like "butterfly-ness" and "gossamer essence"?

I posed this question in presentations and classes and seminars for many years, and there weren't a lot of people who chose answer b.[3]

The fact of the matter is that neither of the pictures is a butterfly. What they are, instead, are representations of a butterfly. Analogs to a butterfly. Artifacts of a butterfly. Proxies for a butterfly.

---

3. And I have my doubts about the truthfulness of those who did.

A SIMILAR LOGIC APPLIES TO THE INTANGIBLES.

The instant we think about, talk about, or write about them, we are no longer truly dealing with the Intangibles themselves. We are only dealing with representations/analogs/artifacts/proxies. The words we use are the nets and the chloroform and the pins and the mattes and the frames. There is inevitable loss similar to what we might think of in our tangible/mechanical world as friction loss or the attenuation of a signal over time and space or the loss of resolution between an original image and a photocopy.

That's the nature of "Intangibleness"; there will always be such loss. With that constraint in mind, let's now imagine a "Spectrum of Intangibility," with the two representations of a butterfly anchoring either end. (Halfway in between might be a live butterfly in a laboratory setting.).

SPECTRUM OF INTANGIBILITY
("Butterfly-ness")

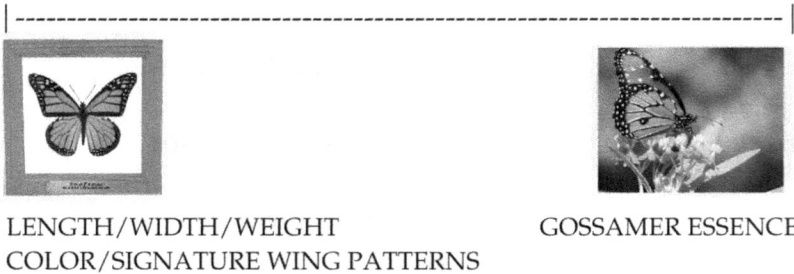

LENGTH/WIDTH/WEIGHT   GOSSAMER ESSENCE
COLOR/SIGNATURE WING PATTERNS

Now let's consider three final questions:

1. Since words are the raw material we must use when attempting to deal with the Intangibles, and since there is always some loss of fidelity or resolution accompanying the use of those words, doesn't it stand to reason that we should

strive to gain and preserve clarity and insight as to the
meaning of the words we are using?

2. Since the words we use will determine just where on the
   Spectrum of Intangibility we are operating, doesn't it stand to
   reason that we should take great care in choosing those words,
   as well as the tone and context in which we use them?

3. Since many (most?) of us are far more comfortable operating
   on the tangible plane, doesn't it stand to reason that we have a
   bias pushing us toward the left-hand side of the spectrum?
   And that we should make a conscious and explicit effort to
   exert a countervailing force to push things appropriately
   rightward?

Those are the questions we'll be examining in the pages that follow.

2 MAYBE WE NEED A NEW WORD FOR ENGAGEMENT

Employee Engagement is an undeniably good thing. The research demonstrating the business benefits realized by achieving a higher degree of Engagement is solid and compelling. Increases in profitability, productivity, growth, and employee retention rates—all are very good things themselves, and all are closely correlated with increased levels of Engagement.

As a matter of fact, doing what you can to ensure that those higher levels of Engagement are achieved ought to be your primary goal as a leader; it's the *What* of the people part of the leadership challenge.

THERE'S A TRAP LURKING OUT THERE, THOUGH, AND IT CAN PREVENT ORGANIZATIONS FROM REALIZING THOSE BENEFITS.

To help you avoid this trap, let me describe an experience I once had while working with a client. She was a corporate vice president who was preparing for an offsite meeting for the top 150 leaders in her company, and she had asked me to look over a copy of the draft agenda and provide some feedback.

The agenda items were pretty standard and straightforward: the just-closed quarter's business results...projections for the remainder of the fiscal year...updates on some key improvement projects...results of the latest employee opinion survey. Those sorts of things.

"At first glance," I said to her, "these certainly seem like sensible enough things to be covering in a meeting like this." But then I pointed to some words that she had penciled in. "I notice that you've added 'Small Group Breakouts' here in the 1:00-3:00 time slot. What are people going to be doing during those breakouts?"

"We haven't decided yet," she replied.

Her answer caught me by surprise. "Then how do you know that breakouts are the best use of this time?"

Now it was her turn to be surprised. "We always have a breakout module in these meetings. We have to get people engaged." And when she said this, her tone suggested a sort of what-turnip-truck-did-this-guy-just-fall-off-of bewilderment. Because in her mind, breakouts equaled Engagement.

But while breakouts might be a good vehicle for facilitating Engagement, they aren't, in and of themselves, Engagement. To understand why that is, let's try a thought experiment.

Imagine two adjacent rooms in a conference center.

Here's a snapshot of the activity in Room A.

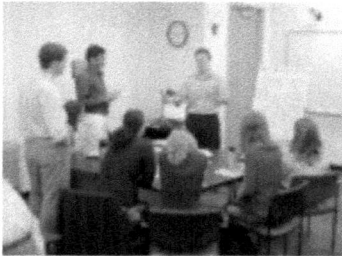

And here's what's going on in Room B.

Question: In which room are the people more highly engaged?

Once again, I posed this question over the years in hundreds of workshops and seminars to thousands of people, and the response was always immediate and virtually unanimous: "Room A." Almost nobody said Room B. Occasionally—*very* occasionally—I'd spot someone whose body language suggested uncertainty, and I'd draw out a third answer:

"Doesn't it depend?"

Which, as it happens, is the correct answer. Why? Consider two scenarios based on what's going on in those two rooms.

SCENARIO 1

The people gathered around the flip chart in Room A are dealing with a topic that is of significant importance to the business and is also right in the mainstream of their day-to-day responsibilities. While they know there is no guarantee that any of their recommendations emerging from this activity will be accepted, they also know that their recommendations will be taken seriously, that they will have been listened to.

At the same time, the people in Room B are being subjected to death-by-PowerPoint. The topic isn't particularly relevant to them, and a Google search on the speaker's name coupled with the words "Grand National Toastmasters Champion!" is unlikely to come up with any hits.

In this scenario, it's safe to assume that, yes, the people in Room A are indeed more engaged.

But now let's consider…

SCENARIO 2

The people in Room A all have the chance to speak their piece as the scribe diligently bullets their comments onto the flip chart. If it's a particularly high-powered breakout session, sticky notes and colored dots may even be involved.

But while all of this is going on, the thoughts running through people's heads are: "Didn't we just go through this exercise a couple of months ago?" And: "There's no way any of the higher-ups are going to pay attention to anything we come up with." And: "This is just a waste of time and paper. I *knew* I should have clicked on Decline when I got the meeting invitation!"

Meanwhile, the speaker in Room B is covering a topic that may seem at first glance to be a familiar one, but he's doing so in new and thought-provoking ways. He's causing people to become actively aware of the assumptions they've been operating under when dealing with the topic, and he's challenging them to consider the validity of those assumptions. He also happens to be skillful enough to be able to hold the attention of a roomful of people seated auditorium-style on the kind of molded plastic chairs generally found in bus stations or at the DMV.

Who's more engaged in this case? Right. The folks in Room B.

ENGAGEMENT IS A COMMON WORD, GENERALLY USED TO CONNOTE SOME FORM OF INTERACTION OR CONNECTION.

When two gears come together, they are said to engage. When a leader holds an offsite meeting with her team to kick off the new process improvement project, she puts a checkmark in the engagement column of her project plan.

And both of those seem like absolutely proper and sensible uses of the word. Here's the problem, though. The Engagement being talked about in the research showing the correlation with dramatically improved business results is a very different thing. *That* kind of Engagement can be defined thusly:

*The extent to which a person invests incremental energy and
effort in the task at hand*

It's not that the energy/effort definition is better than the interaction/connection definition, it's just that it's different.

At this point you might be thinking: "OK. Fine. It's different. But aren't you just making a semantic point?" As a matter of fact, yes, I'm making a semantic point. But—WARNING: SECOND SEMANTIC POINT DEAD AHEAD!—I don't think the word "just" applies here. As Mark Twain famously observed, "The difference between the almost right word and the right word is really a large matter. It's the difference between the lightning bug and the lightning."

Why is obsessing over definitions "a really large matter" when it comes to Engagement?

Consider our leader who always included breakout sessions with offsite meetings. Before deciding to go this route, her thought process might have been this:

> *I want to achieve the kind of energy/effort Engagement that the
> research says will lead to better business results. One interaction/con-
> nection Engagement technique that can be effective in achieving such
> energy/effort Engagement is to bring everybody together for an offsite
> at the beginning of the project. Another interaction/connection
> Engagement technique is to include breakout sessions as part of that
> offsite. So that's what we'll do!*

And if that's what she was thinking, then we're good. But—let's be honest here—it's much more likely that her thought process went something like this:

> *This Engagement stuff is supposed to be important. We better have an
> offsite. And it's gotta include breakouts.*

Could this result in a higher level of energy/effort Engagement? Perhaps. But it could also lead to the kind of cynical reactions— "What a waste of time. I should have clicked on Decline!"—described in Room A, Scenario 2 above, where people are dutifully going through the motions while simultaneously rolling their eyes and sneaking looks at incoming texts and emails on their phones. Said another way, it could cause people to, ironically enough, *dis*engage energy/effort-wise.

The same argument can be made regarding the painfully boring Room B speaker in Scenario 1. In his mind, what he had to say was important, his logic was unassailable, and his PowerPoint slides represented a precise and comprehensive display of that unassailable logic. But he left his audience cold, because in preparing what he was going to say, he didn't give due consideration to how important and/or relevant it was to his audience, to what *meaning* it might have for them.

THERE ARE VARIOUS MODELS USED TO ILLUSTRATE ENGAGEMENT.

While the details of the models differ, they share a common character-istic—the need to account for both the rational and emotional dimen-sions of the human animal.

To be sure, the impulse toward interaction/connection Engagement is a perfectly sensible one. With more opportunities for interaction and closer and more direct connection, information can be communicated more crisply and clearly. Questions can be answered more directly, and the ability to follow-up—and read body language—can ensure that the question being answered is the one that is actually the one being asked. Cycle times can be reduced, since the pertinent facts that people need to do their jobs don't have to work their way through the normal and often byzantine communications channels. And the reduced level of friction loss resulting from this more direct connection will increase the likelihood that the information being received is closer to the infor-mation that was intended to be transmitted.

What it comes down to is this: The currency of Rational Commitment is **Information.** So, if the problem you face can be correctly stated as follows…

We are not getting the right information to where it needs to be when it needs to be there.

...then connect and interact away.

But what if that's not the problem? What if the question that people need answered is not, "What do I need to know?" What if instead, it's, "Why should I care? What does all of this mean to me?"

What happens in such cases is the sort of thing that happened in Room A, Scenario 2. There was plenty of information flowing, facilitated by all of that interaction and connection. (Hell, there were even sticky notes and colored dots!) But there was also a lot of eye-rolling and smartphone checking and regret over not having clicked on Decline when the meeting invitation had arrived.

Something essential was missing for the people in Room A, Scenario 2: meaning. Why is this so critical to Engagement? Because the currency of Emotional Commitment is **Meaning**. People want meaning from their work. They crave meaning. They thirst for it.

So, the propelling question should not be: "How can we ensure more interaction/connection?" Rather, it should be: "How can we ensure that we do the things necessary to bring meaning to the other person?" Not to put too fine a point on things, but answering that question ain't easy. It certainly requires more thought and attention than simply penciling in the words "Small-Group Breakouts" on a meeting agenda.

Here's a (semantic) tip: *When the words "engage" or "engaged" are used as transitive verbs—verbs that take an object—a red flag should go up for you.*

You hear it all the time:

"I've instructed Ellen to engage Greg so that she has the benefit of his insight and expertise."

"Before moving on to phase 2 of the project, we fully engaged the leadership team."

And so forth. But Engagement is not a series of activities in which people participate. It's a feeling state in which people exist. There's a difference between what happens inside a room in a conference center and what happens inside the heads of the people inhabiting those rooms, and there's also a difference between mechanical, procedural inputs and the levels of energy and effort such inputs can generate. Those differences map precisely onto the differences between the two kinds of Engagement discussed above; that's why such usage should be a red flag for you.

> *Engagement is not a matter of leaders engaging employees.*[1] *It's about leaders creating the conditions necessary for employees to be more fully engaged in their work.*

Interaction/connection Engagement is important. In virtually all cases, the ability to achieve high levels of energy/effort Engagement will require the dutiful application of interaction/connection Engagement techniques. The trap lies in assuming that by achieving interaction/connection Engagement you have *therefore* achieved the kind of energy/effort Engagement that will yield all of those wonderful business benefits. It's the *therefore-ness* that's the problem!

Keeping all those interaction/connection and energy/effort references clear is tricky. Which is why I think that what may be needed is a different word to describe what this important but elusive topic is all about. After all, we don't want to be spending a lot of that precious effort and energy parsing the difference between interaction/connection and effort/energy.

What should that word be? We could finesse things by using phrases like "Real Engagement" or "Engagement, Properly Understood," but those are pretty clunky formulations. If there were only an "i" in

---

1. "Engaging" is used as a transitive verb-form in that sentence. Did a red flag go up for you when read it?

"engagement" we could come up with a clever(?) rubric like: "You can't spell 'engagement' without 'm-e-a-n-i-n-g.'"

I don't know what the word or phrase should be. What I do know, though, is that the act of searching for it can help instill a deeper, sounder understanding of what employee Engagement—the kind of Engagement that all of those research results are referring to—actually is. The Engagement that, ultimately, is the *What* of the leader's people challenge.

As Mark Twain might have put it, that would be a very large matter indeed.

————

KEY TAKEAWAYS ABOUT ENGAGEMENT

Engagement: The extent to which a person invests incremental energy and effort in the task at hand

- Engagement happens in people's heads and hearts, not on a flow chart or a meeting's agenda.
- To create real Engagement, therefore, you should not be asking yourself: "How can I connect—or connect with— people in a mechanical way?"
- Rather, you should be asking: "How can I create connections that will help bring meaning to people's work?"

3 YOU CAN'T BESTOW EMPOWERMENT

As a leader, you know that you will be able to accomplish far more through employees who are empowered than employees who habitually seek approval or permission before taking any action. But Empowerment can be an elusive concept in practice.

I once observed a senior leadership team listening intently as the vice president of human resources reported on the findings from a survey designed to measure Empowerment levels throughout the company.

The results were disappointing, and the team's concern was obvious. The business unit's president seemed most concerned of all. He was usually a stickler for staying on agenda, but when the fifteen minutes allotted for this discussion had come to an end, he said: "I know our time's up, but this is important. Let's keep at it."

Thirty minutes later, the president finally called time out. His reluctance was obvious when he said, "We've got to move on to other things." He turned to his vice president of quality: "It's clear that we've got some process problems that are causing people to think they're disempowered. Get your best Six Sigma people on it. Have them identify those process problems and pull together teams to fix them."

Then he turned his attention to his full team: "Let me be as clear as I can be. You are all empowered. I need you to go back to your people and make sure they know that *they* are empowered too!"

From my vantage point in the back of the room, I could see that, for just an instant, the vice president of marketing looked like he wanted to say something. Just as quickly, though, he decided not to. When the meeting adjourned, I managed to get a private moment with him. "You looked like you were about to speak up."

He nodded.

"What was it you wanted to say?"

"I wanted to say that we can tell our people they're empowered until we're blue in the face, but if people don't feel empowered, then they're not empowered."

"Why didn't you say it?"

He furrowed his brow and shook his head. "Nope," he said. "Too risky."

Empowerment is not something that is bestowed, generously handed down from the more rarefied levels of an organizational chart in a gesture of corporate *noblesse oblige*. Rather, it is a sense of assuredness that people at all levels have as they do their jobs. Here is a definition that captures that sense:

> *A feeling of safety while exercising judgment on the job*

Let's parse things a bit more finely.

1. EMPOWERMENT IS A *FEELING* THAT THE OTHER PERSON HAS, NOT AN ASSERTION MADE BY THE LEADER.

To tell people "You are empowered!" is reminiscent of the old joke about the commanding officer telling the troops: "All liberty is cancelled until morale improves!"

The marketing VP's instincts told him that he should speak up. He didn't say anything because he thought it would be too risky; he didn't feel safe enough to do so. In other words—and ironically—he didn't feel sufficiently empowered to question the boss's directive about Empowerment.

2. EMPOWERMENT IS A FEELING OF *SAFETY*.

One clue to just how empowered people feel is the kind of questions they're asking themselves when the time comes for them to take action.

They probably feel reasonably empowered if they're asking themselves questions like these:

- Have I done my due diligence?
- Is my decision consistent with our strategy?
- Is it aligned with our business goals and our mission?
- Is it up to the highest standards of responsible and ethical behavior?
- Does it accurately reflect our values?
- When all is said and done, is this the best decision I can make for the business?

But here's a question suggesting a considerably lower degree of empowerment:

- Will the boss rip my face off?

Granted, that may sound a bit melodramatic. But I have heard those exact words used by people—*senior* people—who had been so beaten down by such treatment over the years that they felt like they had to look over their shoulder when choosing between Coke and Pepsi in the company cafeteria.

The "rip my face off" example may be extreme. The feeling behind it, though, is not so uncommon at all.

3. EMPOWERMENT COMES INTO PLAY WHEN THERE IS *JUDGMENT* TO BE EXERCISED.

Here's a concern about Empowerment that many leaders feel, though don't always voice: "I'm afraid that what starts out as Empowerment will turn into anarchy."

But Empowerment doesn't mean "anything goes." It has to do with exercising judgment on the job. And the most basic judgment is knowing whether or not the situation calls for judgment in the first place. You can't violate company policy and then explain the issue away by saying, "I felt empowered to do it."

In the course of a business day, people face a constellation of situations in which they may need to exercise judgment regarding what to do.

Empowerment is not a one-size-fits-all proposition.

As a leader, you have to make judgments as to just where the boundaries of Empowerment are for each individual on your team. Let's say a team member has worked with you on numerous projects over the years, and you've always found her to be utterly credible and reliable. You feel safe trusting her judgment in widely ranging circumstances. She gets a lot of green lights.

Another of your team members, though, might not come up to such high standards. He's a perfectly capable, perfectly competent employee. But there are certain circumstances in which you feel you need to keep a tighter grip on the reins. You might want him to check in with you as he's moving through his decision-making process. In other words, he gets some yellow lights. Or maybe checking in isn't enough. You might want to approve the call before he makes it. Those are red lights.

THE KEY POINT HERE IS THAT BOTH TEAM MEMBERS CAN STILL FEEL FULLY EMPOWERED AS LONG AS TWO CONDITIONS ARE MET.

First, they have to be clear as to where the boundaries are: what's green, what's yellow, and what's red.

The second condition has to do with what happens when someone operates within those boundaries, but—as happens in the real world—things just don't turn out according to plan, i.e., a green light that didn't go so well.

Let's go back to the melodramatic extreme. If things don't turn out according to plan, and the leader rips the person's face off…well, let's just say that the selection panel for the *Empowering Leader of the Year* award won't be dropping by any time soon for a site visit.

Here's a far more empowering reaction: "You did your due diligence and made a decision according to your best judgment. It didn't turn out the way we had hoped it would. It happens. Judgments aren't infallible. Let's find some time tomorrow to talk about whether or not there were any early warning signs we might have missed."

Of course, if things "not turning out according to plan" becomes a pattern, then the leader has a judgment to make. It may be time to rein things in a bit more—green to yellow, yellow to red.

But as long as there is clarity as to where the boundaries are and reasonableness and professionalism when things don't go according to plan, a feeling of Empowerment can be preserved.

At this point, you may be asking yourself: Isn't this all just leadership 101? Yup, it is. The tricky part about Empowerment isn't that it requires mastering a new and complex set of principles. What's tricky is keeping clear in your mind the powerful connection between the diligent application of those Leadership 101 principles and the extent to which people feel truly empowered.

That picture comes sharply into focus more quickly and easily when you are predisposed to take a step back and consider the world from the point of view of the other person. That will keep you from adopting an Empowerment strategy that consists of louder and more frequent assertions of: "Don't you people understand that you are empowered?!"

In the process, you'll also find yourself spending less time trying to solve the mystery of why people are so reluctant to forge ahead without feeling the need to ask permission, because they will then feel sufficiently safe to do so.

———

KEY TAKEAWAYS ABOUT EMPOWERMENT

Empowerment: A feeling of safety while exercising judgment on the job

- Empowerment is a feeling that a person has, not an assertion that another person makes.
- Ambiguity and inconsistency are the enemies of Empowerment.
- Ask yourself: "Am I being clear about setting expectations?"
- And: "Am I being consistent when it comes to judging performance relative to those expectations?"

4 TOWARD A MORE PRACTICAL DEFINITION FOR "TRUST"

A s I wrote in chapter 1, the reason that this book has focused so much on words and shadings of definitions is that the words we use determine just where we're operating on the Intangibility spectrum introduced in that chapter, and that in turn determines how effective we can be in attending to whichever of the Intangibles we happen to be dealing with at the moment.

In chapter 2, I argued that Engagement tends to be equated with things like wider and broader communication and increased opportunities for interaction. These are familiar notions right out of the canon of Good Leadership Stuff, things that we can point to and count and measure. So we're more comfortable when dealing with them, and as a result, we're more inclined to actually *do* them, placing us firmly on the left-hand side of the Intangibility spectrum.

But Engagement, properly understood, has to do with a feeling of investment in the task at hand. There's a fair amount of gossamer essence in that definition. So while all that increased communication and interaction may help lead to higher levels of Engagement (note: that's "may" not "will"), they are merely potential means to the end, not the end itself. It's only when we get out of our comfort zones by embracing the gossamer essence of Engagement that we can begin to move a few critical millimeters rightward on the Intangibility spectrum.

The pattern is the same with Empowerment, as discussed in chapter 3. The going-in assumption tends to equate Empowerment with two things: 1) granting permission for people to exercise judgment on the job; and 2) communicating to them that permission has in fact been granted. But it's only after embracing the more gossamer definition—a feeling of safety while exercising judgment on the job—that we begin to move those few critical millimeters rightward.

THIS CHAPTER IS ABOUT TRUST, WHICH PROVIDES US WITH A DIFFERENT SORT OF CHALLENGE.

Let's be honest. There is a sense in which Engagement and Empowerment feel like contrivances cooked up at a human resources retreat. You may even remember a time when Engagement and Empowerment hadn't yet made it into the leadership lexicon. So when those words began to pop up on our screens, they might not have been thought of as important new conceptual breakthroughs as much as they were seen as the latest Next Big Thing being foisted on us by HR, which goes a long way toward explaining why nudging them rightward along the Intangibility spectrum involves such heavy lifting.

But we've heard about Trust all our lives. We've heard about it from our parents, our teachers, our clergy, and our mentors. We know in our heart of hearts that Trust is a concept that is big and deep, and that when we deal with it, we're dealing with the real stuff vis-à-vis the Intangibles.

So unlike with Engagement or Empowerment, we already *know* that Trust belongs over on the right-hand end of the Intangibility spectrum.

And it's precisely *because* we know that it's a real, no-foolin' Intangible that we are much more at a loss as to just what to do with or about it.

That's not a comfortable feeling. So we do some checking around to see how others might be handling things. Since it's not very politically savvy to admit to such shortcomings, we keep this investigation pretty low key. But as we gradually poke our heads out from our foxholes a bit further, it slowly dawns on us that no bullets are flying, since pretty much everybody else feels the same way.

This in turn leads to a kind of tacit collusion in fostering a shared belief that: "Hey, it's the soft stuff—the people stuff—that's the hard part. We're doing what we can but..." We may punctuate this by raising our eyebrows and turning our palms up in a "Whataya gonna do?" shrug before reverting to where we're more comfortable—lengths and widths versus gossamer essence.

In order to be able to check the Trust box on our Intangibles action plan, we might add a catch-the-blindfolded-colleagues-as-they-fall-backward-off-a-stepladder exercise to our next staff meeting. Or maybe employ a "Tell us all something you've never told to anyone before!" icebreaker.

Whereas with Engagement and Empowerment we don't really feel all that guilty about cheating over to the left side, since we know those things are just contrivances cooked up by HR, we do feel at least a pang or two of guilt when the Intangible we're talking about is something as profound and important as Trust.

- Deep down, we know that a thing like Trust is important.
- But we feel discomfort at the prospect of having to actually deal with such soft stuff.
- We see a way out in the form of some perfectly reasonable, perfectly plausible action steps.
- We take those steps, updating our PowerPoint decks to reflect the progress(?) that we've made.
- Although we know, deep down, that we haven't really gotten to the heart of things...we take solace in the fact that nobody

else seems to have done so either, because, after all, it's the soft stuff, and everybody knows that it's the soft stuff that's the hard part.

Which brings us to a key point. A lot of things in life—especially in organizational life—come down to presumptions. Presumptions give us a jumping off point...a default position if you will.

SO I'LL POSE A QUESTION: SHOULD YOU, PRESUMPTIVELY, TRUST YOUR COWORKERS?

My answer may seem counterintuitive, but here it is: I don't.

If I find myself heading up a project team, and one of the members of that team—Person A—is someone whom I have never met much less collaborated with, am I going to "trust" that when Person A assures me that "I will do X by Y-date," that it's going to happen that way— especially if X is a mission critical component of the project? No, I'm not. I'm going to build in an appropriate number of checkpoints with Person A along the way to Y-date to ensure that things are proceeding on course.

On the other hand, if Person B gives me the equivalent kind of assurance, and there is a long history of Person B having delivered on such assurances, then I may decide that I don't need as many checkpoints along the way. I will presume to have a higher degree of Trust with Person B than I will with Person A.

Here's the definition of Trust that I recommend:

A feeling of confident expectation

Like Engagement and Empowerment, Trust is a feeling, i.e., something that cannot reside at the far left of our spectrum. But while we know that instinctively, we also know by now that if things get too far right-ward, an equally strong instinct will snap us back over to the left. Fortunately, the other two key words in this definition— "expectation" and "confident"—provide a limit to how far rightward we need to move.

An expectation can be a very specific, knowable, pin-down-able thing. Think of the contract you signed when you took out a car loan. It was essentially a litany of what the parties entering into that contract could expect:

- The number of dollars and cents you would pay each month
- The date on which you would pay that certain number of dollars and cents each month
- The address to which those dollars and cents would be sent
- The acceptable form of that payment: cash, personal check, bank check, electronic funds transfer
- What would happen if you were to fail to meet any of these stipulations
- What sort of indemnification you would have if the car were not to perform to acceptable standards
- A clear description of what those acceptable performance standards were
- Etc.

Of course, before you even got to the point of signing such a contract, the entity providing the funds for that loan—a bank, a credit union, the financing arm of the car's manufacturer—would have looked into your credit history. If it's good, you would receive the standard terms and conditions. If it's less good, you may have to pay a higher rate, if you get the loan at all.

Said another way, the financer would need an acceptable degree of confidence that you would live up to the expectations delineated in the contract. "Confident expectations" having been established, the financer would have a sufficient degree of "Trust" that the loan was a good one to write.

I once did some work for a company that did half of its business outside the United States. One of the fundamental questions that it would always consider before entering into such an international contract was this: "Is there a legal system in place to which we can appeal if the terms of the contract are abrogated?" If so, the sales effort would proceed. The very existence of that functioning legal system would increase the degree of confidence in the contract, i.e., the set of mutually agreed upon expectations. If not, then the contract, as the saying goes, might not be worth the paper it was written on. While they might not walk away from the potential business opportunity, they might find other ways to ensure that they remained whole.

Think back to the trivially simple example where Person A assured me that "I will do X by Y-date." In the limit, I could have lawyered-up and developed a binding contract that included very specific criteria for what "do X" meant as well as a very precise definition for "by Y-date": by "Friday, April 18, 2025, 5:00 p.m., Greenwich Mean Time."

Of course, we don't do this in our day-to-day dealings with co-workers. It would be a terribly inefficient way to run a business, not to mention creating a rather unhealthy working environment. On the other hand, whether or not I accepted those "do X by Y-date" assurances depended on whether or not I was confident that Person A was up to the task, based on either my past experience or the recommendation of others who might vouch for Person A's reliability in such circumstances. And for this to work, I would have to trust (i.e., have confidence in my expectation for) the judgment of that person who vouched for Person A. Not for nothing, but this sounds pretty similar to the kind of formal due diligence that the bank did before giving you the car loan.

We enter into these kinds of implicit contracts all the time on the job. Trust—a feeling of confident expectation—is what's left over when the implicit contracting is done.

Yes, it's an Intangible, which means that, much as we'd like to, we can never move things all the way over to the left on our spectrum. But while Trust itself is an Intangible, the three steps listed below are not. Follow them, and you'll have a better handle on things related to Trust.

I'll leave you by reinforcing this notion:

Trust should *not* be given presumptively, but it can be *earned*.

We'll circle back to this later. Just chew on it for a bit now.

―――――

KEY TAKEAWAYS ABOUT TRUST

Trust: A feeling of confident expectation

So…how to create an environment of Trust?

Three steps:

1. Adopt a more practical definition of Trust: *a feeling of confident expectation.*
2. Ensure clarity regarding expectations, i.e., just what is meant by "do X" and "by Y date." (NB: this is the responsibility of *all parties* entering into this implicit contract. Everyone benefits if all of the pin-down-able things have indeed been pinned down.)
3. Do your due diligence to ensure that you have an acceptable degree of confidence that your expectations will be met.

5 TOWARD A MORE PRACTICAL DEFINITION FOR "RESPECT"

Pretty much all of the qualifiers I made about Trust in the last chapter apply to Respect in this one.

As with Trust, we've heard about Respect all our lives.

As with Trust, we already know in our heart of hearts that we're dealing with the real stuff vis-à-vis the Intangibles and not something cooked up by HR.

As with Trust, we already know that Respect belongs over on the right-hand end of the Intangibility spectrum, so we feel that much more at a loss as to what to do about it.

And as with Trust, we participate in that same tacit collusion: "Hey: it's the soft stuff that's the hard part. Whataya gonna do?"

I once had a client who wanted to address the matter of respect, so he thought it would be a good idea to make eight-foot-high, three-dimensional letters—R-E-S-P-E-C-T—and have them line the drive leading to the company's main entrance. "People will see them every morning when they drive in!" he enthused. Since I knew him pretty well, I felt reasonably safe in offering this suggestion in reply: "Why don't you just hire Aretha Franklin and be done with it?" He got the point.

HERE'S ANOTHER ATTEMPT THAT I WITNESSED FIRST-HAND.

It was a large company that had gotten disturbingly low scores on an employee survey when it came to Respect. So they launched a formal effort to boost those scores. (So far so good. Sorta.) They even went so far as to create a video with substantial production values; as a large company, they could afford the hefty price tag that comes with such a production. (We're still sorta good.) The point the video was designed to drive home is that it's important to acknowledge the presence of others. (Still looking kinda good.)

The video showed a typical conference room with seven or eight people seated at the table. The man at the head of the table—presumably the boss—began the proceedings by saying: "Before we get into our formal agenda, I'd like to acknowledge the presence of a new team member. So-And-So has just transferred over to our team from the Thus-And-Such department. Let's make him feel welcome." At which point all the others either turned or reached across the table to So-And-So from Thus-And-Such, introducing themselves while offering a welcoming handshake.

This is not so good at all. Why not? Because while it is certainly a good thing to introduce oneself in such circumstances, doing so is just a matter of common courtesy. And therein lies the rub.

There's a principle from the legal world that I think applies here:

Expressio unius est exclusio alterius.[1]
The expression of one thing is the exclusion of the other.

A video saying that Respect is a matter of common courtesy doesn't dig anywhere deeply enough. We know in our heart of hearts that Respect is a much bigger deal than that. "But," we tell ourselves, "corporate spent the big bucks on the video, and I showed the video at my

---

1. At last, those four years of high school Latin come in handy.

staff meeting after which I used the talking points provided with the video to facilitate a discussion as instructed, so…" It's at this point that we might swipe our hands together in the universally understood gesture for: "That takes care of that. Done and done!"

The company that used the video as part of their Respect initiative would say that there was a lot more to it than that. But high-production-value video, plus talking points, plus instructions on how to use them in a staff meeting represents some rock-hard tangible stuff that has the effect of pushing us leftward on the spectrum. And like a kid on a swing, we're all too happy to accept the push.

THE SAME ARGUMENT APPLIES WITH RESPECT AS IT DID WITH TRUST, AND I THINK IT BEARS REPEATING HERE.

Whereas with Engagement and Empowerment we don't really feel all that guilty about cheating over to the left side since we know those things are just contrivances cooked up by HR, we do feel at least a pang or two of guilt when the Intangible we're talking about is something as profound and important as Respect.

- Deep down, we know that Respect is important.
- But we feel discomfort at the prospect of having to actually deal with such soft stuff.
- We see a way out in the form of some perfectly reasonable, perfectly plausible action steps.
- We take those steps, updating our PowerPoint decks to reflect the progress(?) that we've made.
- Although we know, deep down, that we haven't really gotten to the heart of things…we take solace in the fact that nobody else seems to have done so either, because, after all, it's the soft stuff, and everybody knows that it's the soft stuff that's the hard part.

I ended the chapter on Trust with this critical point:

Trust should *not* be given presumptively, but it can be *earned*.

I asked you to chew on it for a bit, saying that we'd be circling back to it. Well, we're circling back to it now, because...

Whereas Trust should *not* be given presumptively, but it can be *earned*...

Respect *should* be given presumptively, but it can be *lost*.

I don't, presumptively, give the other person my Trust, and I explained why in the previous chapter.

What I *will* give to any person is my Respect, and I will give it regardless of what that person's pay grade is, what that person's background is, or what that person's demographic profile is. In other words, I will give it presumptively. I have a difficult time imagining anything less appropriate—and more damaging to the organization's soul—than treating people disrespectfully until such time as I have deemed them worthy of my Respect. Until they have—and I shudder to even type these next three words—*earned* my respect.

There's no getting around it. We know that Respect is a certified big deal, that it's a real, no foolin' item on the list of soft stuff. But we like dealing with things that are more rock hard and tangible. We might even say that we find ourselves caught between a rock and, if you will, a soft place.[2]

Here's the dictionary definition of Respect that captures that big-dealness of our dilemma:

Esteem for or a sense of the worth or excellence of a person

Yep. That sounds about right. But it's also about as gossamer essence-y as it gets.

---

2. Or you might even say this if you couldn't resist making a really lame joke.

Let me offer a more practical definition of Respect that I think will help us resolve the dilemma:

Giving due consideration to the other

Let's slice things a little more finely:

- Definition of "the other": *Anybody who isn't you*. That goes for anyone, at any time, at any grade level, in any role in your organization or in your division or on your team with whom you might interact (or, for that matter, outside of your organization).

- The words "the other" sound a little odd, a little discordant, in this context, don't they? Wouldn't it be less awkward to say: "Giving due consideration to others" or "to other people"? Yes it would, and that's the problem. Those phrasings conjure up images of groups of people. The image we need to conjure up is that of an individual person, i.e., an "other."

- "Consideration" means just that. While you were saying or doing whatever it is that you said or did, did you stop to think about—did you *consider*—the effect it would have on the other? If so, great. If not, not so great. But the power of this definition is that it puts the measurement right where it belongs: in your head and in your heart and soul. You may be able to BS your boss, but it's difficult to BS yourself. (Although some people do manage to pull this off, which, though not particularly admirable, can be quite impressive to behold.)

- The word "due" is an important one. It's what keeps things from moving too far rightward on our spectrum. It recognizes the fact that we live in an imperfect world, one that calls for judgments and trade-offs. It also shifts the focus from concepts like "esteem" and "self-worth" to "effects on the business."

AN EXAMPLE.

Suppose you received the following email from your boss in reply to an email you had sent him:

NOT what I was looking for!!

That's it. No further explanation or context. Just those six words and exclamation points, all bold-faced and italicized. What would you do in such a situation?

Well, if you had a really good working relationship with your boss, one that was informed by years of working together, you might have felt comfortable walking down to his office, standing in the doorway until you caught his eye, holding a copy of the email at shoulder height by your thumb and forefinger and saying: "Having a bad day, are we?" At which point he might say, sheepishly, "Yeah. Sorry. I read your report right after returning from a pretty contentious meeting with *my* boss. You were the unlucky one who happened to be in the firing line at that moment."

You'd say OK, perhaps pointing out that the phrase "firing line" is never a welcome one when coming from one's boss. You and he would have a brief discussion to determine why what you had sent him had come up short. He would tell you that he had wanted you to include the latex purchases from Vandelay Industries, at which point you would go back to your office and realize that all you now had to do was copy-paste part of a document that you had saved—it was in the Penske File—and that would be it. Crisis averted. Case closed.

But now let's consider another scenario. You get the same email, but the working relationship with your boss is less than hunky-dory. Under the circumstances, you conclude that this would not be the most propitious time to have an exploratory conversation with him.

So you decide to take another cut at things. It's probably going to take you the rest of the day to get this done. You check your calendar and see that your regular weekly staff meeting is scheduled from 1:00-4:00, so you send out a calendar revision to your staff, moving the meeting to the following afternoon. Your calendar now cleared, you dig in on the repair work for your boss.

You spend the afternoon on that repair work and send it off to your boss before leaving for home at the end of the day. Much as it pains you to have to do this, you keep your phone close at hand through the evening.

Sure enough, an email from your boss arrives at 9:43 p.m. It begins: "No!" Not a good sign, notwithstanding the fact that this time, at least, it was not in all caps, bold faced, and italicized. And there was just one exclamation point. Fortunately, there was more to the message: "I thought we said we were going to include the latex purchases from Vandelay?"

You stop and think—*Aha! The Penske file!*—then fire up your laptop, copy-paste the relevant section, and send it off to your boss. When you get up the next morning, you check your email. Yup, there it is, in your inbox. You (anxiously) open it: "Thanks." Crisis resolved. Case closed.

Using our practical definition of Respect—*giving due consideration to the other*—who in this scenario was being disrespectful?

Your boss, of course. Had he taken a moment to think about how his original email would be received, he might have included the bit about Vandelay Industries. By not doing so—i.e., not giving it due consideration—he chewed up your afternoon, thereby driving down your efficiency and productivity. Such are the business costs of such disrespectful behavior (not to mention an erosion of Trust).

Was anyone else being disrespectful? Well, if when you decided to move your staff meeting all you did was send out a calendar revision —no explanatory note—weren't you being disrespectful? Didn't this amount to doing the same thing to your people that your boss had done to you—summarily changing how they would be spending their afternoons both today and tomorrow? After all, they're responsible professionals too. Presumably they had planned out productive uses for those times.

And wouldn't this have caused a ripple effect for still other people with whom they had planned on meeting the next afternoon? Now think of the penalties in efficiency and productivity that can accrue to the business as this ripple expands. And how people will file this experience away in their memories, to be consulted on some later date when determining the degree of confident expectation—a.k.a., Trust—they will have in future dealings.

At this point you might be thinking: "In the real world, stuff happens. Things change. If someone is so rigid as to not be able to adapt to such changes, then maybe they've got some soul searching to do."

And this is where the "due" comes in. Under the circumstances, you may not have had any choice but to spend the afternoon working on your boss's priority. But had you stopped to think about—to consider —the fact that your moving the meeting would be affecting "the other," you could easily enough have added a brief explanatory note to the meeting update: "Sorry for the last-minute change, but I just got pulled onto an urgent project that will take up my afternoon. I've moved the staff meeting to tomorrow. Holler if this is a problem. Thanks for your understanding."

You can rationalize all you want to, but it doesn't absolve you from failing to take the time to give due consideration to the fact that what you do affects other people, individuals who have their own sets of issues and challenges and conflicting responsibilities to face while doing their jobs. At the very least, you as their leader can stop and take a beat if it will avoid making things even more challenging than they have to be.

I'll have much more to say about Respect in a later chapter (Spoiler alert: It's sort of the key to all this Engagement stuff.).

FOR NOW, LET ME OFFER A FEW CLOSING THOUGHTS.

Had I pulled in to work one day and been met by a series of eight-foot-high letters spelling out RESPECT as I proceeded to the parking lot, and then attended an 8:00 a.m. staff meeting that began with a video that seemed to reduce Respect to a matter of introducing myself to new colleagues in meetings like the one I was sitting in at that very moment, I might have thought: "Boy am I glad that I work for a company that is serious about Respect."

- But here's what I would be more likely to be thinking: "That video wasn't about being 'respectful.' It was about not being a very bad word that rhymes with 'brass pole.' I'd rather they save the money spent on the video and the Stonehenge reproduction now lining the driveway and put it into a training program titled: 'How to stop screwing up productivity by jerking around people's calendars.'"

- Here's a much shorter—and far more ironic—way to say this: I would have felt disrespected. And I bet I wouldn't have been the only one to feel that way. The urge to take action is a fine and necessary one. It's a place of business, not a faculty lounge. But our more practical definition of Respect— "giving due consideration to the other"—adds an essential step to the process. It forces us to ask: "How will what I am about to do impact other people?" The asking of the question, along with a good faith effort at answering it, can save you from some serious missteps.

Let's suppose you were determined to make a video about the recent outbreak of "failure to display common courtesy by introducing oneself to new team member" behavior you were experiencing. Wouldn't it have been more effective to show things from the point of view of the new person at the meeting? Show him sitting at the table, feeling the kind of awkwardness we all feel when we're the new kid on the block? Maybe get a close-up of him with a voice-over of the thoughts running through his head: "Should I introduce myself? Or would that disrupt the meeting?" Or: "I'd like to make a point here, but I feel kind of funny doing so." And so on.

- By showing things from an observer's point of view, the focus —and the attendant lesson—was on the activity of introductions and handshakes. "Giving due consideration to the other" puts the focus where it belongs: not only on what we might do—or as is the case here, what we might *not* do— but on its effect on the other.

This is important, so I want to circle back to it again:

Trust should *not* be given presumptively, but it can be *earned.* Respect *should* be given presumptively, but it can be *lost.*

Respect *can* be lost, and care should be taken—every day, as it happens —not to lose it. But everyone, regardless of rank or title or whatever other factor you might want to consider, is entitled—yes, *entitled*—to Respect (i.e., due consideration) as a basic condition of employment. To think otherwise is to invite the creation of the kind of Hobbesian environment—nasty and brutish—in which no business, much less its people, can survive for long.

———

KEY TAKEAWAYS ABOUT RESPECT

Respect: Giving due consideration to the other

- Respect should *always* be presumptively given.
- Above all, Respect has to do with keeping in mind how what you do—or do not do—affects the other person.
- The word "due" in that definition is important. It keeps things reasonable—but you can't use it as a cheat!

6 A WIDELY HELD—AND FALSE—DISTINCTION

Several years ago, I was asked to develop a one-hour "Intangibles" module to be added to a company's three-day training program for new leaders, i.e., those who had just been promoted into positions that would have them managing people for the first time in their careers. To get a good sense of the context where the to-be-developed Intangibles module would be used, I sat in on the delivery of the program in its then-current state as an observer.

The guest speaker near the end of the program's third and final day was Jeff, an executive who had just completed a two-year tour of duty as the aide de camp to Wayne, the company's CEO. Jeff's presentation was excellent. He was able to take many of the theories and principles covered during the program and show how they had real-world application at the highest levels of the company. Judging by the attendees' attention level, you might even say that they were fully engaged.[1]

Toward the end of his session, Jeff posed the following question: "What percentage of Wayne's time would you estimate he devotes to 'people matters'?"

---

1. See scenario 2 in chapter 2.

The answers were all in the fifteen to twenty percent range. Jeff nodded, assuring all that their guesses were perfectly reasonable before hitting them with his punchline: "On a typical day, Wayne spends about fifty to sixty percent of his time on people matters. That leaves him with just forty to fifty percent to focus on the business." At this, the thirty or so new leaders raised their eyebrows, shook their heads ruefully, and exchanged significant glances while dutifully scribbling notes in their program binders.

After offering a few closing remarks, Jeff gave a humbly grateful wave as he exited the room to enthusiastic applause. I was seated at the back of the room near the exit, so as Jeff passed me, I quietly arose and walked out of the room with him.

"Got a second?" I asked.

"Sure," Jeff replied.

I had gotten to know Jeff reasonably well from some previous work I had done with him, so I felt safe in offering a well-intentioned critique.

"That was terrific," I began, honestly. "But you said something toward the end that could have had the effect of undermining your message a bit."

"Oh, dear," he said, genuinely concerned. "What was that?"

"You said that because Wayne spent fifty to sixty percent of his time on people stuff, he could only spend about forty to fifty percent of his time 'on the business.'"

Although he was too polite to say so, Jeff's expression said it for him: "Yeah? So?"

"By phrasing it that way, you implied that time spent on the people stuff is *not* time spent 'on the business,'" I replied.

He gave a puzzled wince.

I attempted an explanation. "You had just spent the better part of an hour making a compelling case for the importance of the people side of the leader's job, and the way you did it was spot on. But by wording things the way you did at the end, you put the people part of things over here"—and I gestured to my left—"and 'running the business' over here"—and I gestured to my right.

The light went on for Jeff. "*Now* I see what you're getting at," he said. I felt relieved. I shouldn't have.

"I see it, but I don't agree with it," he continued. "I think you're splitting hairs, John. *They* got the message." He pointed over his shoulder to the classroom from which we had just emerged. Then he looked at his watch: "I've really gotta run. Maybe we can pick this up later?"

"Sure, sounds good," I said, secure in the knowledge that this follow-up conversation would never happen.

In the years since this scenario unfolded, I have become more convinced than ever that my critique of Jeff's presentation did not represent hairsplitting at all.

As a matter of fact, I'd go so far as to say that the disconnect that I had experienced with Jeff is right at the heart of everything discussed in these pages.

If we operate from the assumption that "the people stuff" is over here and "the business" is over there:

- We might recognize that being good at the people side of things is crucial to business success.

- We might take it seriously by, for example, inviting the CEO's former aide de camp to speak to a group of newly minted leaders about the importance of that people stuff.

- We might regularly survey employees about the people stuff, diligently examine the results, and put into place serious, substantial efforts designed to improve our performance along this or that people-related dimension on which we had come up short.

- We might, when the hoped-for improvements don't occur, redouble our efforts with even more serious, more substantial, and more best-practices-focused efforts.

- But if things still don't measure up even after all of those redoubled efforts, we have left ourselves with a handy escape hatch: "I've really gotta run. Maybe we can pick this up later?"

Here's another way to look at things.

- We do indeed have a business to run.

- One hundred percent of what happens in the running of that business flows from what is done (or not done) by people. The business *is*, therefore, the sum total of the actions taken (or not taken) by those people.

- The effectiveness of those actions depends on the degree to which those people are engaged, i.e., the extent to which they bring the full measure of their skills, wisdom, experience, effort, and energy to the tasks at hand.

- This is fundamentally and profoundly affected by leader's skill / facility / acumen at attending to the people stuff, the Intangibles, a.k.a., the "soft stuff."

- Given all of the above, separating "the people stuff" from "running the business" represents a false distinction.

- Disabusing ourselves of that false distinction is Step 1 along the path to getting a firmer handle on employee Engagement and the rest of those elusive Intangibles.

Why is taking this first step so critical? Because it welds the escape hatch shut. It prevents us from adopting that all-too-familiar pose—palms up, shoulders shrugged, head cocked thirty degrees to the side, eyebrows raised, lips pursed tightly in regret—before invoking that all-purpose exculpatory mantra: "It's the people stuff. Whataya gonna do?"

There are historical precedents demonstrating how welding shut such escape hatches can lead to dramatically improved business results.

HISTORICAL PRECEDENT 1: TOTAL QUALITY MANAGEMENT

In the 1980s and early part of the '90s, Total Quality Management—TQM—was all the rage. This didn't happen because of leaders' sudden desire to achieve a platonic level of goodness in their business dealings. It happened because they were getting waxed competitively. Over time, dramatic and sometimes breathtaking progress was made in applying the principles of TQM. But before that could happen, some long-standing assumptions had to be challenged.

Pre-TQM, the abiding mindset was this: "Of course quality is a worthy goal, but people are imperfect, and entropy exists. So some number of defects will inevitably occur." Or said another way: "Whataya gonna do?"

Operating from this mindset, businesses put in place a number of things to help mitigate that inevitability:

- Quality departments, staffed by white-coated professionals armed with meters and calipers and clipboards.

- Incoming inspection processes designed to weed out bad components and materials before they polluted the production line.

- As products became ever more complex, ever more

sophisticated pieces of Automatic Test Equipment (ATE) emerged to help identify those inevitable defects.

- Repair and rework loops salvaged the value inherent in assemblies and sub-assemblies that had failed in-process inspections.

- Explicit declarations of Acceptable Quality Levels (AQLs), the precise to n-significant-digits level of defects that would be tolerated.

All those quality departments and calipers and pieces of ATE and rework loops and AQLs carried with them not inconsiderable dollar costs. But—Whataya gonna do?—defects are inevitable. And besides which, that's the way we'd always done things, we'd been successful at it in the past, so there was no compelling need to change.

Then Japan happened. Or more precisely, Japanese businesses began diligently applying the teachings of two Americans, W. Edwards Deming and Joseph M. Juran, the Ruth and Gehrig, respectively, of the quality movement.

What had been a mark of poor quality, a label reading "Made in Japan," became the new gold standard as breakthrough improvements were made.

Essential to such breakthrough results was the adoption of three principles that challenged the abiding conventional wisdom:

1. A goal of a sound quality strategy must be to prevent defects from occurring in the first place as opposed to inspecting to identify defects after they had already occurred.
2. In the limit, the goal should be zero defects.
3. The fundamental unit of analysis should not be defects; rather, it should be the process that yielded such defects.

If ever the expression "prophets without honor in their native land" was a fitting one, it applies to Drs. Deming and Juran. There was nothing in what they taught Japanese industry that had not already been available—and that they had not already been preaching—for decades, to American and other Western businesses. Unfortunately, the abiding mindset in the West said: "Sure, that stuff might work in Japan. But things are different over there. And besides which, things are going along pretty swimmingly with the way we've been handling quality around here, so we'll take a pass."

Here's the thing: The very existence of the things that represented "the way we do quality" were the cause of our inability to understand the existential threat posed by the new conventional wisdom as espoused by Deming and Juran.[2] All those clipboards and calipers and ATE and AQLs and repair-and-rework loops had the effect of blocking our line of sight to a much better and far more profitable way of doing things. The cacophony created by all of that misguided activity drowned out the wisdom contained in the teachings of the good doctors.

At the root of it all? A presumptive "Whataya gonna do?" attitude.

HISTORICAL PRECEDENT 2: JUST-IN-TIME INVENTORY (JIT)

Even with our newfound wisdom vis-à-vis quality, we were in a transition period. We may have adopted prevention as our fundamental quality strategy as opposed to inspection. Philosophically speaking, we may have accepted that a goal of zero defects was doable. And we may have begun focusing far more of our attention on the process that caused the defect rather than on the defect itself.

But until we reached that desired level of performance, some defects would still be occurring, some rework loops would still be necessary, and some mitigating strategies would still need to be in place.

---

2. And, to be sure, others.

One of those mitigating strategies was the carrying of additional inventories of raw materials, parts, subassemblies, assemblies, and even finished products to offset those still-inevitable defects. And even if there were no quality issues to contend with, surely economies of scale and the discounts associated with volume purchases would argue in favor of the need for carrying nontrivial inventories of parts and raw materials, wouldn't they?

As it happens, no, they wouldn't.

For one thing, all of that inventory carries with it substantial costs: the cost of the inventory itself, the cost of the physical plant needed to store that inventory, the cost to insure those assets, the cost of the people needed to manage and process and handle them, and so on. At the risk of stating the obvious, added costs erode competitive position.

Not only that, but the existence of that excess inventory and the systems to support it added a substantial inertial load to business operations. If one assumed steady state conditions, this was less of an issue. But as markets became more and more dynamic, that inertial load made it more difficult to manifest the kind of nimble and agile performance necessary to be competitive in those ever-faster-moving markets.

Enter Just-In-Time inventory—JIT—the first principle of which is this: Businesses should carry no inventory other than just the amount needed, where it's needed, when it's needed.

This posed what seemed to be a dilemma for even those practitioners who might be open to considering the adoption of JIT practices: "While I can see the validity of such an approach in theory, it can only work in practice if we have utter reliability in the quality of the parts and materials that are being delivered where and when they're needed, whether they are coming from upstream in our own production process or from external suppliers. Since we are not yet at that point, how can we reconcile theory with practice?"

That seems like a sensible and prudent response. As it turns out, though, there is no dilemma. and JIT principle number two explains why: Excess inventory does not insulate you from the effects of quality problems. Rather, it insulates those problems from their solutions.

A metaphor that's often invoked in discussions of JIT is that of "draining the swamp." While on the surface things may look placid and picturesque, at the bottom of the swamp are stumps and reeds and abandoned cars and other slimy unpleasantness. It's only after the swamp is drained that the slimy unpleasantness is revealed.

In the JIT metaphor, the excess inventory being carried is represented by the water. By eliminating inventory—that is, by "draining the swamp"—many more causes of quality problems are revealed than had previously been visible, and we are shaken out of the false sense of security that we were lulled into by that placid, picturesque surface view of things.

Eventually, dramatic progress was made as more and more businesses applied the principles of JIT. As with TQM, such progress would never have happened without a willingness to not be limited by long and deeply held assumptions.

In both cases, the systems and practices put into place based on those assumptions had the effect of blocking out lines of sight to deeper solutions, and the cacophony created from those systems and practices had the effect of drowning out the wisdom of those who had already seen the light.

HISTORICAL PRECEDENT 3: LEAN

Over time, the insights at the heart of JIT led to what we now refer to as Lean, in which the bar has been further raised, from the elimination of excess inventory to the removal of all excess process steps, i.e., steps that do not "add value."

After such dramatic progress made on the factory floor represented sufficient proof of concept, analogous steps were taken and breakthroughs realized in office and administrative processes, and then out to direct interaction with customers.

It was not just an accident of fate that these advances had their genesis in the eminently practical and tangible world of manufacturing. A broken or out-of-spec widget is something that can be seen and touched and measured. The dollar costs associated with all that plant and equipment and inventory are large and obvious, and they translate boldly and directly to the bottom line.

But while the effects of less-than-ideal performance may be less direct in office or customer-facing environments, even administrative processes can be mapped. And there is nothing in the least abstract about an angry customer at the other end of a telephone line or pulled onto the shoulder of a highway awaiting assistance.

Making the translation to the Intangibles, though, remains as a major challenge since, by definition, they cannot be seen or touched or directly measured. That will be the topic of our next chapter.

By way of setting the stage for that discussion, here are a few questions for your consideration:

- What is an employee survey if not an inspection?
- What are low survey scores related to the Intangibles if not defects?
- What is our presumptive willingness to expend effort to mitigate low employee survey scores if not what might be thought of as "safety stock of 'time inventory'"?
- How sure are we that all of the steps we go through in such mitigation efforts are, net, adding value?
- Could all of the programs and processes we're implementing in order to improve our results vis-à-vis the Intangibles actually be blocking our line of sight to the real issues? And drowning out the voices of those attempting to call our attention to those real issues?
- And, finally, what will we find if *that* swamp is drained?

7 DRAINING THE SWAMP: SOLIPSISM, RESPECT, AND EMPLOYEE ENGAGEMENT

Before answering the final question I posed at the end of the last chapter—what will we find if *that* swamp is drained?—there's a related question that needs to be considered.

Why is the water so deep? What is shielding our view of the problem at the root of our inability to achieve higher degrees of true employee Engagement?

Quite a few things, actually:

- The research reports and conferences and articles purporting to identify "best practices" when it comes to attending more effectively to the Intangibles.

- The processes and protocols and procedures we've put into place as part of past and well-intentioned efforts to implement those best practices.

- The PowerPoint presentations we've generated and metrics we've tracked and rewards and recognition systems we've instituted to nudge people toward the kinds of behaviors that we understand to correlate to those best practices.

- And above all, the imprecision and inconsistency in the understanding and usage of words and terms associated with employee Engagement and other key Intangibles.

If I'm going to be perfectly honest about things, I have to concede that this book may well have poured a few more liters of water into the swamp:

- For one thing—and to invoke a highly technical term—it contains a lot of stuff.

- Moreover, the effectiveness of all this stuff is limited by my all too considerable shortcomings as a writer.

- As I wrote earlier, there is inevitably going to be some loss of precision and clarity when using mere words to capture the essential characteristics of the Intangibles, since words are the tools we have at our disposal to make a rational case about something that exists on a plane that is orthogonal to things rational.

To mix the swamp metaphor with the metaphor introduced previously, the "water" that fills "the swamp" is all those netted/euthanized/matted/framed butterflies that we've collected when what we're really trying to get at is the "gossamer essence" of the thing.

NOW THAT I'VE GOT YOU THOROUGHLY CONFUSED WITH ALL OF THOSE SWAMPS AND BUTTERFLY NETS AND GOSSAMER ESSENCES, LET'S TRY A THOUGHT EXPERIMENT.

Suppose that Engagement and Empowerment and Trust did not exist. Or to be a bit more precise, let's stipulate that while those Intangibles do exist, we haven't yet recognized them as rising to the level of concepts that we've decided to label and describe and discuss and do something about.

Suppose that the only such Intangible that we have so identified and labeled is Respect, properly understood. Now let's introduce a convention to be used throughout the rest of this book. For our purposes, **RESPECT**—all caps, bold faced—will signify **RESPECT** properly understood to mean: Giving due consideration to the other.

Why single out **RESPECT**? Because it differs in kind from the others. It is the only one over which each of us has full control. No permission is needed before you can give due consideration to the other. No company-wide initiatives are necessary for you to manifest **RESPECT**. No incremental resources are required. Rather, it is entirely up to the individual—at any time, on any day—as to whether or not he or she will infuse **RESPECT** into whatever circumstances are at hand.

Unlike **RESPECT**, the other Intangibles we've discussed are not directly within an individual's control. Rather, they are the result of other things having been done well.

- It's great to have people offering the full measure of their effort and energy to the tasks at hand, i.e., be Engaged…

- …and it's great to have people feel safe while exercising judgment on the job, i.e., be Empowered…

- …and it's great to have people manifest confident expectation when interacting with coworkers, i.e., be informed by a sense of Trust.

Whether or not any of those things happen, though, depends upon many, many factors well beyond any individual's immediate control. They are outputs, not inputs. They are destinations to be reached, not the fuel that will get you there.

RESPECT is an input. **RESPECT** is that fuel.

HOW MIGHT HAVING A CLEAR LINE OF SIGHT TO RESPECT MAKE THINGS BETTER?

Consider the case of the corporate vice president in chapter 2. As you will recall, she was preparing for an offsite meeting for the top 150 leaders in her company, and she had asked me to look over a copy of the draft agenda and provide some feedback. Here's a recap.

> The agenda items were pretty standard and straightforward: the just-closed quarter's business results, projections for the remainder of the fiscal year, updates on some key improvement projects, results of the latest employee opinion survey. Those sorts of things.

> "At first glance," I said to her, "these certainly seem like sensible enough things to be covering in a meeting like this." But then I pointed to some word she had penciled in. "I notice that you've added 'Small Group Breakouts' here in the 1:00-3:00 time slot. What are people going to be doing during those breakouts?"

> "We haven't decided yet," she replied.

> Her answer caught me by surprise. "Then how do you know that breakouts are the best use of this time?"

> Now it was her turn to be surprised. "We always have a breakout module in these meetings. We have to get people engaged." And when she said this, her tone suggested a sort of What-turnip-truck-did-this-guy-just-fall-off-of bewilderment.

But suppose that instead of being guided by a need to "get people engaged," she had been guided by a need to ensure that the agenda was viewed as a way of infusing maximum **RESPECT** into the proceedings. Had that been the case, her penciled-in notation to the agenda might have been more like this:

- Who are the people that will be attending the meeting?
- What is important to them?
- What is most likely to resonate with them?

Bear in mind that **RESPECT** means giving "due" consideration to the other. The VP had some solid business objectives for the meeting, so it wasn't a matter of making sure the agenda was sufficiently entertaining for the attendees. Had that been the case, she could have just hired some singers and dancers, some acrobats and jugglers, and been done with it.

With **RESPECT** as the informing notion, though, her thought process would have been more along these lines: *I've got three objectives for the meeting. Given the meeting's attendee list—who they are, what's important to them, what will resonate with them—how should the meeting be structured to ensure that it yields the results that I'm after?*

Is that an easy question to answer? Not at all. But a necessary condition for coming up with a serviceable answer to a difficult question is that the question be asked in the first place.

Why, in our thought experiment, would the corporate VP have been more likely to ask just that question framed just that way? Because she would not have been distracted by the concept of Engagement, since, after all, no such concept had yet been identified and labeled.

With no easy out available to her—"We always have a breakout module in these meetings. We have to get people Engaged."—she would have been left with no alternative other than a healthy infusion of **RESPECT**, which in turn would have led to a better business outcome for her.

————

Now let's consider the senior leadership team, as described in chapter 3, as they listened intently as the VP of human resources reported on the findings from a survey designed to measure Empowerment levels throughout the company. Here's that recap.

The results were disappointing, and the team's concern was obvious. The business unit's president seemed most concerned of all. He was usually a stickler for staying on agenda, but when the fifteen minutes allotted for this discussion had come to an end, he said: "I know our time's up, but this is important. Let's keep at it."

Thirty minutes later, the boss finally called time out. His reluctance was obvious when he said, "We've got to move on to other things." He turned to his VP of quality: "It's clear that we've got some process problems that are causing people to think they're disempowered. Get your best Six Sigma people on it. Have them identify those process problems and pull together teams to fix them."

Then he turned his attention to his full team: "Let me be as clear as I can be. You are all empowered. I need you to go back to your people and make sure they know that they are empowered too!"

From my vantage point in the back of the room, I could see that, for just an instant, the VP of marketing looked like he wanted to say something. Just as quickly, though, he decided not to. When the meeting adjourned, I managed to get a private moment with him. "You looked like you were about to speak up."

He nodded.

"What was it you wanted to say?"

"I wanted to say that we can tell our people they're empowered until we're blue in the face, but if people don't feel empowered, then they're not empowered."

"Why didn't you say that?"

He furrowed his brow and shook his head. "Nope," he said. "Too risky."

The business's president was a good man, trying to do what he genuinely felt was best for the organization. Let's consider all of the ways that his approach to the situation at hand had represented the logical and sensible things to do.

- In his mind, he had identified a clear problem statement: "People don't realize that they are fully Empowered."

- The results of the latest survey could not have been more clear on this point, so he was being driven by facts and data, not by gut feel.

- He knew that in the vast majority of cases when there was a problem at hand, it wasn't the fault of people for not doing things right. Rather, it was better to identify the process shortcomings that were causing well-meaning, dedicated people to serve up the undesirable result in question.

- He had people on his staff who were highly trained in this sort of process analysis and intervention: a crack team of Six Sigma experts.

- He gave his VP of quality, in whose reporting chain resided all those experts, clear and explicit direction.

- And he knew that with any such problem, clear communication was essential. So after giving that charge to the quality VP, he had issued an equally clear directive to the rest of his leadership team.

All this was, indeed, highly logical and rational. But Empowerment is an Intangible—a feeling of safety while exercising judgment on the job —that resides on a different plane, one that is orthogonal to the logical/rational plane on which businesspeople like to remain squarely grounded.

> The president's past logical, rational learning about facts and data and best practices and process focus and communications had the effect of blocking his line of sight to the real problem at hand.

All these things represented the sensible, best-practice-certified approach. As an added bonus, it enabled him to bask in the illusion of rigor provided by his comfort zone: "We've got an important problem. I have laid out a clear, sensible course of action. Who could take issue with it?"

As it happens, the VP of marketing could have. But he chose not to. Why not? Because he knew that saying what was on his mind would be like shouting a warning to someone upwind in a hurricane. He wouldn't be heard, and he might get hit by dangerous airborne debris in the process.

Let's now revisit the situation faced by the business unit's president, but this time we'll apply the rules of our thought experiment, where the concept of Empowerment had not yet been identified and labeled, where the only Intangible he had to work with was **RESPECT**. Under that set of circumstances, his charge to his leadership team might have been more along these lines:

"People keep going to their bosses or directly to you—in some cases even to me—when they have difficult situations to deal with. They're always looking for direction—even permission—to do things that they're fully capable of doing on their own.

"This is an inefficient way to run the business. Not only is it more costly for us to be spending our time on things that can be handled by people at lower pay grades, but it also slows things down and keeps us from being as fast and nimble as we need to be."

At this point he might have projected a PowerPoint slide that contained this sentence:

> *Each of us has the responsibility to infuse the organization with* **RESPECT** *every chance we get.*

Then he might turn back to his team and continue:

"You and I may know that our people are capable of doing the work without our direction or permission. If they weren't, they wouldn't be in the jobs they're in. But this isn't about what we know. It's about what they—the 'others'—think.

"You and I may know that we've taken steps to change things. But this isn't about what we've done. It's about how they—the 'others'—have reacted to those things we've done.

"This is tricky stuff...a lot trickier than trying to identify the process step that's causing our widgets to be defective." He might then raise his eyebrows, shrug, and hold out his hands, palms up, in a beseeching gesture, while asking: "Anybody got any ideas on this?"

At which point the VP of marketing might say: "There are times when I hold back, when I'm not sure I have the authority to make a call or to be as candid as I might be."

Here the president's eyebrows might go from raised to furrowed: "Why wouldn't you?"

"Because," might come the marketing VP's reply, "I didn't feel safe in doing so." At which point the cat, as it were, would have been belled.

How realistic is this **RESPECT**-fueled scenario? I don't know. What I do know, though, is that it—or something like it—would be a whole lot more productive than the way the scenario had actually unfolded in the real world.

More to the point, it's a scenario that's a whole lot more likely to occur if it's informed by a felt need to sharpen the focus on the other. If it's fueled, that is, by the need to infuse **RESPECT** throughout the organization at every opportunity. And *that's* a whole lot more likely to occur if the line of sight leading to it is not blocked by a misunderstanding of the concept of Empowerment and the easy out it can provide.

It could be argued, in fact, that things went off the rails as soon as the situation at hand was viewed as "a problem to be solved" as opposed to "a complex situation to be managed." That's because "a problem to be solved" is catnip to anyone whose thought processes skew to the logical/rational, and because that "situation at hand" exists on that other, orthogonal plane.

And that way, as we all know, lies dragons.

––––––

Or consider the scenario about receiving the email from your boss that read:

"NOT what I was looking for!!"

Why might a leader send such an email?

Let's dispose of the easy and obvious answer first: The leader in question is that bad word that rhymes with brass pole. But since this book is not aimed at people who for whom sociopathy is seen as a core competence, we'll move on.

––––––

> For our purposes, it's more interesting—and more realistic—to ask: "Why would a leader who is a good and well-intentioned person send such an email?"

––––––

The likeliest answer is that he or she had had a bad day, was highly stressed owing to all the issues that were slopping over the edges of his or her already full plate and had—to invoke another not terribly elegant term—hosed things up.

It happens. All of us know this. And when it happens, we probably feel remorse for having done such a thing. We might even call the recipient of the email into our office to make amends, which is the right and noble thing to do.

But what if we were able to offload some of the things that were raising the noise levels in our day-to-day dealings? More specifically, what if we could remove the talk-talk-talk and the meetings and the PowerPoint presentations and the survey results and the Lucite tchotchkes that have heretofore gone with our well-intentioned efforts to attend more effectively to the Intangibles, which we know to be important, but—dammit—we've got a business to run and people need to be a little more thick-skinned when we screw up like this, don't they?!

What if—as is the case in our thought experiment—the only Intangible that had been identified and labeled was **RESPECT**, and what if we had a poster hanging on our office walls much like the PowerPoint slide that the business president projected in the Empowerment scenario above:

> *Each of us has the responsibility to infuse the organization with*
> ***RESPECT*** *every chance we get.*

Would we not be considerably less likely to write such an email? Or at least to take a beat before clicking Send?

The power of a more single-minded focus on **RESPECT** has to do with fostering an atmosphere of what we have come to label as Trust, which in turn will help people have a deeper feeling of what we have come to label as Empowerment, which in turn will result in people who are more deeply and fully characterized by what we have come to label as Engagement.

Because all the above will result in higher levels of efficiency, shorter cycle times, lower levels of employee turnover, and a substantially higher ROI to the owners of the business!

This is about business results, not about being good guys or gals. If you happen to be in an industry where sociopathic behavior is seen as a requirement to producing those attractive ROIs, then have at it. If, on the other hand, you work in a somewhat more highly evolved environment, then establishing an ethos informed by **RESPECT** might be the better way for you to go, since **RESPECT** is the fundamental nutrient of organizational health.

———

So...
...if more frequent and abundant infusions of **RESPECT** are what it takes to get this sort of progress

...and if **RESPECT** means "giving due consideration to the other"
...then after the swamp has been drained, what we would find is our tendency to give insufficient consideration to, if not total unawareness of, "the other."

There is a word for this tendency, and that is *Solipsism*:

> *A theory in philosophy that your own existence is the*
> *only thing that is real or can be known*

Granted, Solipsism is kind of an obscure word. Why use it when other, more familiar words such as *self-absorption* or *self-centeredness* are readily available? Precisely *because* it's obscure. (And also because self-absorption and self-centeredness aren't quite synonyms for Solipsism.)

One theme of this book has been the price we pay in our ability to attend more effectively to the Intangibles because of inconsistent and/or imprecise usage of seemingly familiar words, such as Trust and Empowerment and Engagement and, especially, Respect. With Solipsism, we start with a relatively clean slate. We don't have to unlearn the definitions we've been using in the past. As a result, its obscureness becomes a feature, not a bug.

All of which leads me to an assertion:

> *Solipsism—both institutional and individual—is the root cause of our inability to attend more effectively to the Intangibles.*

Institutional Solipsism is the tacit assumption that all that matters is what goes on here at the company. What happens outside these walls is irrelevant. To the extent that it's thought about at all, it's seen as a distraction or an annoyance.

One marker of institutional Solipsism is the term "work/life balance." Think about what that term says: "There's what you do at work, and then there's your life."

But that's not how employees—all those "others" who don't so much as exist in an institutionally solipsistic world view—see things. Their perspective is more likely along these lines: "My job is a part of my life. It's a very important part, but I'm a fully formed adult with family responsibilities, and my work in my community, and my hobbies, etc., etc., etc."

The boss who sent the *"NOT what I was looking for!!"* email back in chapter 5 was likely operating from a pretty solipsistic point of view: "I'm a busy man. I don't always have the time to be diplomatic!"

Please note that the invocation of Solipsism is meant as a diagnosis, not as an indictment. Entropy being what it is, a tendency toward Solipsism is the natural state of things. Where can the countervailing force come from? From constant infusions of **RESPECT**, from adopting the discipline to always give due consideration to the other.

Said another way, Solipsism is the disease; **RESPECT** is the antidote.

RESPECT begets Trust...

...Trust begets Empowerment

...Empowerment begets Engagement

...Engagement begets a greater return on your investment in human capital

...A greater return on your investment in human capital begets a better financial ROI for your shareholders.

Isn't that the way it's supposed to work? Isn't that the point of the exercise? Of trying to get better at the people stuff? At attending more effectively to the Intangibles?

8 ON BEING MORE "OTHER-WISE"

Two notions were introduced in the last chapter. **Solipsism** is a theory in philosophy that your own existence is the only thing that is real or can be known…and the root cause of our difficulty in being able to attend more effectively to the Intangibles. **RESPECT** is properly defined as "giving due consideration to 'the other'" and the antidote to Solipsism.

To this point, the discussion of just what "due consideration to 'the other'" might mean has focused on the effects of what one says (or doesn't say) and does (or doesn't do) on "the other," e.g.:

- The person in chapter 5 who received the *"NOT what I was looking for!!"* email.
- The VP of marketing in chapter 3 who thought that it was too risky to speak up about the way the business unit's president was approaching Empowerment.
- The people in chapter 2 participating in a pointless breakout session and regretting having accepted the meeting invitation in the first place.

There is no question that "due consideration to 'the other'" speaks to such examples and that it's important to consider the effect one is having on "the other." But this raises a key question:

How can you know—in advance—what those effects might be?

Well...

...if being effective as a leader means having a high degree of employee Engagement

...and if the degree of Engagement is a function of **RESPECT**

...and if the degree of **RESPECT** depends on the extent to which you give due consideration to "the other"

...then doesn't it stand to reason that you will have a better sense of what those effects might be if you know who "the other" is...what matters to him or her...what makes him or her tick...what will resonate with him or her...

...and, most important of all, could it be that owing to a high degree of institutional Solipsism, you might not be giving due consideration to the potential *positive* effect that the other might have on the business... that he or she might have some life experience that falls outside the bounds of your job descriptions and process maps but could add substantial value to your efforts...that they might even have had a good idea or two that was developed while working in a building that did not have your company's logo on the door?

Consider a hypothetical. Suppose all a leader's followers are exactly like the leader in every way. They think the same way. Their learning style is the same. Their likes and dislikes are the same. Their strengths and weaknesses are the same. And so on and so forth.

How well would such a leader "know" her followers? Pretty well. In this case, giving "due consideration to 'the other'" would probably boil down to making sure that their names were spelled correctly on their paychecks.

Now let's consider a far less hypothetical example—the president of a corporation presiding over a leadership team meeting in the 1960s. How well did he (and it would have been a he) know the members of that leadership team? Quite well. They were pretty much all fifty to sixtyish-year-old, white, Anglo-Saxon Protestant males.

But that's no longer the world in which we live. Now the "due" in "due consideration" brings with it many more factors, such as age cohort, gender, sexual orientation, ethnicity, degree of ableness, and so on.

Does being attentive to such demographic categories represent a higher order of "due consideration"?

It can. But it can also represent a kind of enlightenment on the cheap. Why on the cheap? Because those categories are objective and measurable. They represent a way of doing something about the people stuff without having to stretch any conceptual muscles since it fits our rational/tangible bias.[1]

CONSIDER TWO FOLLOWERS ON AN ORGANIZATION CHART.

Jim is a twenty-eight-year-old epileptic, bisexual male of Armenian ancestry.

Gladys is a sixty-one-year-old mother of three and grandmother of six whose parents immigrated to the US from Ireland, has been married to her high school sweetheart for forty-two years, attends daily Mass, and whose sexual orientation we do not know because, as she puts it, "It's none of your g**d*** business!"

---

1. This is why some people have philosophical concerns about the extent to which formal diversity efforts focus on demographics. They get a jolt of cognitive dissonance caused by an instinctive sense that something deeper is being missed.

Do we now know some useful and important things about Jim and Gladys? Yes, we do.

Do we know enough to know just what the "due" in "due consideration" means for each of them? No. Or at least not unless we are going to make judgments based on stereotypes.

Which brings us right to angst-provoking Ground Zero of the Intangibles. Because we know we need to know it. We know that it's important. We know that it's what makes effective leaders effective. And we know that it's bloody hard to do.

Human nature being what it is, easy is more attractive than hard. If there's an easier way out—an escape hatch—we'll use it.

By equating diversity with demographics, by commissioning the construction of eight-foot-high, three-dimensional letters spelling R-E-S-P-E-C-T to line the entry road to the employee parking lot, by making videos that equate Respect with a handshake and a "Hi, nice to meet you."

We use those escape hatches to avoid having to actually come to grips with the true nature of the challenge at hand—if, that is, it were possible to grip something that's intangible.

Even as we crawl through those escape hatches, though, there is a part of us that, deep down, knows that we're avoiding something important, that we're copping out.

And that's where that angst comes from.

THE ONLY REASON THAT BEING EFFECTIVE AT ATTENDING TO THE INTANGIBLES IS IMPORTANT IS THAT IT WILL LEAD TO BETTER BUSINESS RESULTS.

Said another way, the reason the soft stuff matters is that it has a big effect on the hard stuff.

Now, it is an economic truism that "most interesting things happen at the margin." Other things being equal, whoever is able to offer an additional increment of value to the customer—a bit of added value *at the margin*—will win out.

In the '80s and '90s, that marginal advantage redounded to companies that were the earliest to get religion about TQM. A decade or so later, that edge went to those who diligently and effectively applied the principles of JIT. Still later, those who applied the principles of Lean to a fuller range of business processes—including those outside of the factory—gained the competitive edge.

By now, though, pretty much everybody knows and has applied those principles. (Those who haven't have been left behind, if they're still in business at all.) The reason there has been so much attention paid in recent years to things like Engagement is that we have come to sense—not quite know but sense—that Engagement is where the source of competitive advantage now resides. We've done the value-added flow analyses and process-improvement projects—the hard, tangible stuff—and we've reached the point of diminishing returns. We kinda/sorta know that—are afraid that?—the marginal edge is now going to have to come from the soft stuff, from being better at attending to Engagement and other key Intangibles. And we're right. Engagement *is* the critical *What*.

Dealing with the Intangibles has always caused a fair amount of discomfort. Knowing that such uncomfortable subject matter will now be the terrain on which competitive battles must be fought won't help.

Higher levels of employee Engagement *should be* your objective—the *What*, if you will; the research is clear and compelling on that point. Tapping into higher levels of effort, energy, and expertise that your employees have to offer *will* increase the return on your investment in human capital.

Will this be easy to do? Hell no. But remember: You don't have to be perfect at it. You just have to be better. Better than you were yesterday and better—at the margin—than the competition.

9 A BRIEF DILATION ON "ENGAGEMENT" AND "VALUE"

n the preface to this book (and, for that matter, in its title) I said that the argument for effective leadership I was going to make in its pages could be summed up thusly:

If Engagement is the What, Then Respect is the How.

But if we parse things a bit more finely, first with this definition…

Engagement: The extent to which a person invests incremental energy and effort in the task at hand

…and then with this one ..

Respect: Giving due consideration to the other

…there's a question that's still left hanging:

Just how does "giving due consideration to the other" increase the extent to which that other person invests more "incremental energy and effort in the task at hand"?

In other words: *How does one implement the "how"?*

WHICH BRINGS US TO THE CONCEPT OF VALUE.

If there is one thing that I think I learned[1] during my thirty-or-so years limping around the consulting circuit, it's that what motivates people is the pursuit of Value.

- Customers want to maximize Value received.
- Shareholders want to maximize Value received.
- Vendors want to maximize Value received.
- And, yes, employees want to maximize Value received.

Which brings us to yet another definition. From an individual's point of view…

$$\text{VALUE} = \text{What-I-Got/What-It-Cost-Me}$$

Or put more simply…

$$\text{VALUE} = \text{GOT/COST}$$

So for customers, the GOTs that they receive are the product plus service plus various—yes—intangibles, such as peace of mind or status. The COSTs are the purchase price plus repair and maintenance costs plus opportunity costs plus such intangibles as buyer's remorse.

For shareholders it's pretty straightforward. When all is said and done, they will hope that they GOT a lot more money than they invested, i.e., their COST. (There are, of course, also intangibles in a shareholders' Value calculations, most having to do with tolerance for risk.)

It gets rather more complicated when we think of what represents Value for employees.

---

1. I say "think I learned" out of a well-founded sense of humility.

On the GOT side of the ledger are things like a fair day's pay for a fair day's work, job security, comfortable working conditions, the collegiality that goes with being part of a team, a reasonable possibility of career growth, and so on.

The COSTs include the daily grind of setting your alarm for 6:00 a.m., the two-way gridlock-fighting commutes, the missed dinners and children's school plays or ball games when you have to work late,[2] and—let's face it—the frustrations that go with being part of a large, complex organization where your point of view might not be honored, if it's given a hearing at all.

I'm not going to suggest that there is a simple, or even complex, algorithm into which you can plug some numbers and come up with a value-maximizing answer for your employees.

Nor am I saying that customers, shareholders, or employees actually sit down with paper and pencil and actually do their own GOT/COST calculations. Yes, they may make lists of pros and cons in a given situation, but in no way do they explicitly plumb the depths of all factors that add up to what yields Value for them in the way I've defined it here.

Rather, I'm saying that it's a sense that simmers and roils and ultimately synthesizes in a person's head and heart as a result of living through—of feeling—those various GOT and COST factors.

As a leader, having a feel for what those GOTs and COSTs might be—i.e., what Value might be—for a given employee is a difficult question to answer. But as I wrote in chapter 7, "(A) necessary condition for coming up with a serviceable answer to a difficult question is that the question be asked in the first place."

---

2. Granted, this has been mitigated somewhat by the work-at-home movement that emerged from the Covid-bred Zoom phenomenon.

Nor am I suggesting that the GOTs and COSTs will be the same for each employee. But trivial as it might sound, knowing your employees a bit better as people will make you more likely to have scooched a bit closer to the answers as well.

And just so there's no confusion: The goal here is not to be a good guy or gal. It's to achieve higher levels of Engagement among your employees—the What—thereby making you a more effective leader, thereby making the business of which you are a part more successful.

All that said, there is a word that not only represents a synthesis of the various GOTs and COSTs that combine to yield Value for an employee, it's also unique to each employee. It's a word that first came up in the chapter about Engagement,[3] and that word is Meaning. As I wrote: "The currency of Emotional Commitment is Meaning. People want meaning from their work. They crave meaning. They thirst for it."

KEY TAKEAWAYS ABOUT ENGAGEMENT AND VALUE

- Saying that "meaning" represents this wonderful and unique synthesis of all of these Value factors doesn't make *its* meaning easy to discern. It's complex, complex as hell.
- Thinking in terms of what represents the meaning of work to the other person puts you, perforce, on the proper plane from which to give due consideration to the other, i.e., it, perforce, makes you respectful of that person.
- Since being more respectful of the other is the secret to achieving higher levels of Engagement...
- And since achieving higher levels of Engagement is the secret to achieving better business results...
- It would appear to be a worthwhile thing to do...
- Wouldn't it?

------

3. Chapter 2, "Maybe We Need a New Word for Engagement."

10 CONCLUSION: A PERHAPS NOT SO MODEST PROPOSAL

"Simplify, simplify."

HENRY DAVID THOREAU

"One 'simplify' would have sufficed."

RALPH WALDO EMERSON

For decades, businesses dealt with quality issues in the traditional ways that, at the time, represented best practices. Lots of inspection. Lots of rework loops. Lots of additional inventory of parts and materials to make up for the inevitable losses in scrap and rework following all those inspections.

Then somebody said: "All those things that you're doing to solve your quality problems are actually *causing* those problems. They're blocking your line of sight to the real root causes, which reside in your work processes." And enormous progress was made.

For decades, businesses dealt with inventory issues in the traditional ways that, at the time, represented best practices. Stock up to take advantage of volume discounts. Keep enough on hand to supply planned production as well as rework owing to quality issues. Invest in the people and physical plant needed to store and manage that inventory in the best, most efficient ways possible.

Then somebody said: "Your interpretation of the problem at hand is blocking your line of sight to its real solution. All of that inventory is preventing you from realizing the kinds of efficiency and agility to be gained by adopting a just-in-time approach to inventory management." And enormous progress was made.

FOR DECADES, BUSINESSES HAVE UNDERSTOOD THE NEED TO ATTEND MORE EFFECTIVELY TO THE INTANGIBLES.

More recently, the focus has been on the concept of Engagement and the substantial increases in business performance that go with it. Well-intentioned, well-funded efforts have been made and conferences have been held and studies have been done, all of which have had the effect of describing a collection of best practices.

What I am perhaps not so modestly proposing is that all those efforts and conferences and studies and best practices are blocking our line of sight to the root of the problem, that that problem is a tendency toward institutional and individual Solipsism, and that the antidote to Solipsism is Respect, properly understood to mean "Giving due consideration to the other," where that "other" is not a cipher or a face on an employee ID badge, but a living, breathing human being, and where **RESPECT** is the fundamental nutrient of organizational health.

I am not a Pollyanna. I most assuredly do *not* think that if we just showed each other a little more respect we'd all be transported into a world of unicorns and comfy chairs. It isn't that easy.

But it is, in fact, that simple. And simple is hard, as suggested by

Thoreau's famous quote and Emerson's wonderfully ironic reply that appear at the beginning of this chapter.

As a matter of fact, trying to make things simple poses something of a dilemma for me. For the past ninety plus pages, I've been arguing that we have to let go of some of the assumptions we've been making about the Intangibles, to embrace their "intangibleness," to stop thinking in terms of "What to do?" and start first coming to grips with "What effect will they have on 'the other'?"

But unless I provide some specific prescriptive steps, this will all have been an exercise in abstract thinking, which can be nice, but which also won't get you very far.

HERE, THEN, ARE SOME PRESCRIPTIVE STEPS CONSISTENT WITH THIS BOOK'S CENTRAL ARGUMENT.

Stop talking about most of the Intangibles that have been covered in these pages.

- Stop talking about Trust. Instead, think in terms of creating an environment in which it becomes easier for the other to feel confidence in what can be expected from you.

- Stop talking about Empowerment. Instead, think in terms of creating an environment in which the other will feel safe while exercising judgment on the job.

- Stop talking about Engagement. Instead, think in terms of creating an environment in which others will be more likely to bring to bear the full measure of their effort and energy on the tasks at hand.

If you must invoke those words, invoke them as adjectives instead of as nouns. Not "Trust" but "Trusted" or "Trustworthy." Not "Engagement" but "Engaged." Not "Empowerment" but "Empowered." Why?

- A noun is a thing, an entity unto itself: We're over here, and it —the noun—is over there.
  - "We need more 'Engagement.' Let's order some up!"
  - "When will the next order of 'Empowerment' be delivered?"
  - "A new box of 'Trust' just arrived."

- An adjective can't exist by itself. It modifies something else. Saying "engaged" or "empowered" or "trusted" suggests the existence of something else.

- What is that "something else"? A person, i.e., an "other."

- Which is precisely the point. Engagement is not a thing that we do/create. It's something that resides within the other.

- See the difference?

EMPOWERMENT   ENGAGEMENT   TRUST

Start focusing all your efforts vis-à-vis the Intangibles on creating an ethos of **RESPECT**.

- Make sure everyone knows that Respect, properly understood, means "giving due consideration to the other."

- Introduce the concept of Solipsism—both institutional and individual—and make sure others understand its corrosive effect on the culture you want to create.

- Remember that the obscureness of the word "Solipsism" is a feature, not a bug.

- Although I'm not big on slogans and posters...
  - Take advantage of the fact that Solipsism comes with its own built-in slogan that lends itself to a handy shorthand: "SOS—Stamp Out Solipsism."
  - If you must make posters, consider this one:

Metrics are also important, so here's the metric I'd recommend: *The percentage of people who pass The Mirror Test each day.*

- How to implement The Mirror Test:
  - Next to the door/exit of each person's workspace, hang a mirror.
  - Instruct everyone to, before leaving each day:
    - Look into the mirror.
    - Ask yourself this question: "Yes or No: In doing my job today, did I give due consideration to 'the other'?"
    - Record your answer.
    - Go home.

- That's it. Simple to implement. Hard as hell to pass.

———

Back in the introduction, I told my "Piano Man" story and said that it was one of two incidents that have most brightly illuminated the nature of the challenge at hand when it comes to attending more effectively to the Intangibles.

HERE'S THE OTHER ONE.

My assignment had me working closely with Ned, a senior manager in the company's HR department who was responsible for leadership development programs. He had just completed a research project designed to identify those specific behaviors most closely associated with highly rated leadership performance.

The research methodology Ned had employed was simple and straightforward.

- Some 5,000 employees had been surveyed, approximately one-third of the company's entire workforce.

- Included within those 5,000 survey subjects were suitable representations of all functions, all job grades, all demographic categories, and all geographic locations.

- Survey respondents were first asked to rate the leadership effectiveness of the person to whom they directly reported along a 5-point scale, with a rating of 5 meaning *excellent* and 1 meaning *poor*.

- Respondents were then given a list of several dozen generally recognized leadership behaviors and asked: "To what extent does your leader demonstrate each of the following behaviors?" This was also done along a 5-point scale, with 5 meaning *always* and 1 meaning *never*.[1]

Ned then explained to me how he had been able to identify the 10 leadership behaviors most closely associated with the highest-rated leaders. He emphasized that while there has been no shortage of research done over the years for business in general, the fact that this survey had been done exclusively within his company added validity to the results he had gotten. I told him that I couldn't agree more.

But our thinking began to part ways when Ned said the following: "What we need to do now is to develop programs to help leaders get better at those 10 behaviors. If we do that right, our 'leadership effectiveness' results should improve."

"If you do that, you might see improved results," I replied, "but I wouldn't be so sure that you'd be getting at the root of the issue."

"What makes you say that?" Ned asked, with a puzzled look.

"I think you may be confusing correlation with causality,"[2] I said.

At this, Ned's expression changed from puzzlement to displeasure. Hoping to make amends, I added, "It's a common mistake." That didn't help.

Undaunted, I soldiered on. "Your strategy is based on the assumption that if you can get leaders—people who manage other people—to manifest and improve those ten behaviors, they will then be better leaders."

---

1. Behaviors rated included such things as upholding high ethical standards, demonstrating business acumen, setting priorities, delegating, listening, communicating, evaluating performance, resolving conflict, collaborating across functions, etc.
2. For readers who enjoyed our earlier excursion into a dead language, here's the Latinate way of saying this: "Post hoc ergo propter hoc" or, "After this, therefore because of this."

Ned nodded, but it was clear that he was still not 100 percent pleased with the trajectory of our conversation.

I continued. "There's another hypothesis that ought to be tested. It could be that better leaders are the people who are characterologically predisposed to do those ten things. It's that innate characteristic in someone who is a good leader that people sense, not the behaviors themselves."

Now Ned was clearly conflicted. "I hear what you're saying," he said. "But even if you're right, what can we *do* about it?"

"You can delve more deeply into the characteristics of those leaders who were highly rated," I replied.

"But you don't understand," Ned said. "I had a hard enough time getting senior leadership to OK this research. If I go back to them now and say that we have to do more, they aren't going to buy it. This gives us hard data to support programs that can help lead to visible, observable behaviors, things that we can see and point to. What you're suggesting leaves us with nothing we can see, nothing that we can get our arms around."

Exactly so. That eighty-word answer from Ned represents the most succinct, clear-eyed, and heartfelt statement of the core problem at hand that I have ever heard.

Which brings us to a very old joke:

> A man is driving along a city street and comes to a corner. As he makes a right turn, he notices another man on his hands and knees on the sidewalk, under a streetlamp.
>
> The driver stops the car, gets out, and approaches the other man. "Are you all right?" he asks.
>
> "Yes," answers the man on his hands and knees. "I'm fine. I'm just looking for my car keys."

The first man says, "You're pretty sure this is where you lost them?"

"No," says the man on his hands and knees, "but the light's better here."

Taking on the challenge of dealing more effectively in the domain of the Intangibles makes many (most?) leaders uncomfortable. While we understand that it's important, we just find it hard to get a solid grip on such things. And when you think about it, that makes perfect sense, since—by definition—you can't touch an Intangible.

What do we do? We do the things that have made us successful in the past, like chartering teams, and mapping processes, designing and implementing communications plans, defining and tracking metrics, and measuring progress, and making midcourse corrections, and what not. And when we do that, we think that we're doing the best we can vis-à-vis the Intangibles. After all, when we look around, we see that that's what other people are doing, so how far off can we be?

Said another way, we look where the light is better. This is exactly what Ned's instincts were telling him about how to proceed based on the research he had done regarding leadership behaviors.

Trouble is, that's not where the keys are.

One key lies in accepting and embracing the fact that the Intangibles are...intangible. As such, they are orthogonal to the rational/logical issues with which businesspeople are more comfortable dealing.

Another lies in disabusing ourselves of the false distinction between "running the business" and "the people stuff" and recognizing that, in the limit, all a business is *is* its people.

Still another key lies in coming to the humbling realization that pretty much everybody that makes up your business isn't you, i.e., they are all "the other."

Finally, embracing the fact that everything you say (or don't say) and do (or don't do) has the potential to affect those others.

SO, WE FACE A CHOICE.

We can put together teams, research best practices, and perform analyses comparing our historical performance with those best practices and then create project and program plans to improve things vis-à-vis Engagement and Empowerment and Trust and Respect and integrate all of the individual project plans into an overarching master plan which captures in one view where every jot and tittle of each of those individual plans is entered, showing the relative progress of each, thereby enabling us to do a better job of monitoring progress and making any necessary midcourse corrections, all the while realizing that each of those efforts overlaps with all the others, suggesting the need for models and Venn diagrams making clear the relative importance and areas of overlap, thereby enabling us to make now-better-informed midcourse corrections, all the while making sure that we have the systems and metrics in place to recognize and reward people's efforts related to this important work...people, that is, who aren't all the same, calling for even more sophisticated processes and analyses and mechanisms to enable us to account for all kinds of differences in demographic categories and subject matter expertise and life experience and educational and professional background, interjecting at the appropriate times with the results of all-hands surveys, overlaying the results of said surveys onto what we've done to date so that we can make still better midcourse corrections and monitor and measure and improve and recognize and reward...and on and on it goes, at all times doing good, sensible, leadership stuff.

Or we can go down a simpler path than offered by the previous, 250-some-odd-word-long sentence, recognizing that the one thing we can pretty much control is the extent to which people are treating each other with Respect and asking ourselves at the end of each day: Did I give due consideration to the other?

Make no mistake. While that second path may be simpler, it is by far the more difficult one to traverse.

Because along that path, there are no PowerPoint slides or Venn diagrams or Pert charts to hide behind. No cacophonous din to distort meaningful signals into misleading noise. No colleagues to disappoint you by misunderstanding an order or missing a deadline.

There's just you, looking into a mirror, and considering your answer to a simple question—"Did I give due consideration to the other?"— knowing that the answer can only come from someplace within your heart and soul.

Which is as it should be, since that's where the Intangibles, properly understood, reside. That's where the keys can be found.

ACKNOWLEDGMENTS

While, yes, this book is dedicated to her, I cannot write an Acknowledgements section without beginning by citing the contribution that my wife, Gail, made to the writing of this book. Everything that I accomplished in my professional life, especially after life threw me the curve ball that set me down the path toward management consulting—I know that's a mixed metaphor, but you're just going to have to cope—would have been impossible without the love and support provided me by my Gail. I was blessed to have had her in my life for more than forty years. I just wish it could have been more.

My daughter, Joanna, lives just across the New Hampshire border with her husband, Bob. The only thing that surpasses my pride in the career in software that Jo has carved out for herself is the love I have for her. I cherish the times I have with Jo and Bob. They're part of what keep my motor going to do things like write books.

You met my son, Mike, in the introduction. (He was the one who showed up soon after "Piano Man" was playing on the radio on the ride to the hospital.) Mike now lives in New York City with his wife, Kari, and their two young sons. He has had a successful career for nearly twenty years now in the film and TV business as a cameraman. And as boring as it might be to read, I'll write the same about him as I did about Jo. My pride is exceeded only by my love. And spending time with Mike and Kari and their sons—which is to say, of course, my *grandsons*—is a big part of what keeps my synapses firing at something approaching a reasonable rate.

My parents were Harry and Antoinette. No one was ever blessed to have had parents who were more loving and attentive and caring than were mine. I had a warm, happy, Ozzie and Harriet spiced with marinara sauce childhood, and I'm sure that played a significant role in my success, both academic and professional. I thought that such upbringings were the norm. I now realize that they weren't, and I have become all the more grateful to my parents as that realization has sunk in.

My brother, David, a PhD in mathematics from Cambridge University, is a smart cookie. He is also a skilled comedic essayist and playwright, describing himself on his website this way: "Of all post-nineteenth-century mathematical logicians, I claim to be the funniest."

David is clearly among the top two writers in our family. Whenever I write anything, I count on his useful critiques. And no small point, he is also the most honorable man I know. Though it will make him uncomfortable to read this, the same pride-love thing applies with David as it did with Jo and Mike.

I was launched into the world of consulting by the surprising success of my first book combined with being laid off from my corporate job at about the same time. That book was published by Amacom, the book publishing arm of the American Management Association (AMA). I went on to have four books and six training videos published by the AMA. They also sponsored innumerable seminars and keynotes that I delivered—which helped to sell books, which helped to sell videos, which helped to sell other speeches and seminars and books and videos, etc., etc., etc.

This flywheel turned for several years. It was remunerative for me and for the AMA, and I learned an enormous amount throughout the process. None of it could have happened without the efforts of my two main points of contact at the AMA: Ron Mallis and John Doerr. I thank them for what they did for me.

After chasing around the country for the AMA—with the occasional stop in Canada, Europe, or South America—for all those years, I was, to use the technical road warrior's term, gassed. I wanted to find a job where I didn't have to travel as much. So I was probably the first person who ever went to work for a consulting company to *cut down* on travel when I joined Rath & Strong. I had many smart and talented colleagues there, among whom were Meredith Allen, Dave Berlew, Dan Ciampa, Elisabeth Swan, and Tom Thomson. I learned a lot from—and delighted in working with—each of them during my five years at R&S.

Another of my Rath & Strong colleagues was Nort Salz. Nort gets a special mention here because a number of years after I had left R&S, Nort and I teamed up to form a consulting firm named—hold onto your hats: big creative sunburst ahead—Guaspari & Salz. We did... okay. It wasn't a complete disaster, but you wouldn't be inclined to associate G&S with the word "juggernaut" either.

Most important to me, though, is that it's now twenty-some years later, and I still consider Nort to be one of my dearest friends in the world, this in spite of the fact that he is wrong about everything when it comes to politics. (And come to think of it, I'd say that he and my brother are pretty much tied for that Most Honorable Man I Know title.)

Finally, a very large chunk of my consulting career consisted of saying to clients: "You need to think more about your customers' point of view." Sure, there would be variations on that theme, but when you stripped things down to their essence, that's pretty much all I ever said to them. Made a good living doing so, too. This truly is a wonderful country.

All kidding aside, I'd like to acknowledge and thank you for having bought this book as well as all the people who bought my other books or videos, read my articles or columns, or sat through my seminars or speeches. I hope I was able to deliver the value for which you paid, value that was at least equal to what I received from having had the opportunity to serve you.

ABOUT THE AUTHOR

Since the mid-1980s, John Guaspari has helped leaders take on the challenge of being more effective at attending to "the intangibles," with a special focus on the topic of Employee Engagement.

He is the author of seven other books, including the best-selling *I Know It When I See It: A Modern Fable About*

Quality and *Otherwise Engaged: How Leaders Can Get a Firmer Grip on Employee Engagement and Other Key Intangibles*, seven best-selling training videos, and hundreds of articles and columns.

He has worked with hundreds of corporate clients in scores of industries and delivered over a thousand intangibles-related keynotes, seminars, and workshops.

Long before entering the world of consulting, he began his career as an aerospace engineer, after earning a bachelor's degree (Notre Dame) and a master's degree (Cornell) in that field. After a few years as an engineer, he shifted gears and went on to hold corporate positions in such widely varying functions as marketing, customer support, quality, leadership development, and organizational effectiveness.

He lives in Walpole, Massachusetts, a mile-and-a-half from Walpole Country Club, of which he is a member, and at which he continues to play that damnable game until he eventually becomes frustrated enough and decides to toss his clubs into the nearest dumpster and be done with it.

For more of John Guaspari's writings, see his website: **johnguaspari.com**

www.ingramcontent.com/pod-product-compliance
Lightning Source LLC
Chambersburg PA
CBHW032325210326
41519CB00058B/5809